math expressions

Common Core

Dr. Karen C. Fuson

Watch the lemur come alive in its forest as you discover and solve math challenges.

Download the *Math Worlds AR* app available on Android or iOS devices.

Grade **4**

Volume 2

This material is based upon work supported by the
National Science Foundation
under Grant Numbers
ESI-9816320, REC-9806020, and RED-935373.

Any opinions, findings, and conclusions, or recommendations expressed in this material
are those of the author and do not necessarily reflect the views of the National Science Foundation.

Unit 5 | Measurement

BIG IDEA 1 - Converting Measurements

BIG IDEA 2 - Perimeter and Area

BIG IDEA 3 - Understanding Decimals

BIG IDEA 4 - Analyzing Polygons

Student Resources

Dear Family:

This unit includes the metric measurement system. During this unit, students will become familiar with metric units of length, liquid volume, and mass, as well as the size of each when compared to each other.

One **meter** is about the distance an adult man can reach, or a little longer than a yard.

One **liter** is about two large glasses of liquid, or a little more than a quart.

One **gram** is about the mass of a paper clip or a single peanut.
One **kilogram** is a little more than 2 pounds.

Students will also discover that the metric system is based on multiples of 10. Prefixes in the names of metric measurements tell the size of a measure compared to the size of the base unit.

Units of Length

kilometer	hectometer	dekameter	meter	decimeter	centimeter	millimeter
km	hm	dam	m	dm	cm	mm
10 × 1 hm	10 × 1 dam	10 × 1 m	10 × 1 dm	10 × 1 cm	10 × 1 mm	
1 km	1 hm	1 dam		10 dm	100 cm	1,000 mm
= 1,000 m	= 100 m	= 10 m		= 1 m	= 1 m	= 1 m

The most commonly used length units are **kilometer**, **meter**, **centimeter**, and **millimeter**.

The most commonly used units of liquid volume are **liter** and **milliliter**.

The most commonly used units of mass are **gram**, **kilogram**, and **milligram**.

If you have any questions or comments, please contact me.

Sincerely,
Your child's teacher

CC SS Unit 5 addresses the following standards from the Common Core State Standards for Mathematics: **4.MD.A.1**, **4.MD.A.2**, **4.MD.A.3**, **4.MD.B.4**, and all Mathematical Practices.

Estimada familia:

Esta unidad incluye el sistema métrico de medidas. Durante esta unidad, los estudiantes se familiarizarán con unidades métricas de longitud, volumen del líquido y masa, así como con el tamaño de cada una comparada con las otras.

Un **metro** es aproximadamente la distancia que un hombre adulto puede alcanzar extendiendo el brazo, o un poco más de una yarda.

Un **litro** es aproximadamente dos vasos grandes de líquido, o un poco más de un cuarto de galón.

Un **gramo** es aproximadamente la masa de un clip o un cacahuate. Un **kilogramo** es un poco más de 2 libras.

Los estudiantes también descubrirán que el sistema métrico está basado en múltiplos de 10. Los prefijos de los nombres de las medidas métricas indican el tamaño de la medida comparado con el tamaño de la unidad base.

Unidades de longitud

kilómetro	hectómetro	decámetro	metro	decímetro	centímetro	milímetro
km	hm	dam	m	dm	cm	mm
10 × 1 hm	10 × 1 dam	10 × 1 m	10 × 1 dm	10 × 1 cm	10 × 1 mm	
1 km = 1,000 m	1 hm = 100 m	1 dam = 10 m		10 dm = 1 m	100 cm = 1 m	1,000 mm = 1 m

Las unidades de longitud más comunes son **kilómetro**, **metro**, **centímetro** y **milímetro**.

Las unidades de volumen del líquido más comunes son **litro** y **mililitro**.

Las unidades de masa más comunes son **gramo**, **kilogramo** y **miligramo**.

Si tiene alguna pregunta o algún comentario, por favor comuníquese conmigo.

Atentamente,
El maestro de su niño

CC SS **En la Unidad 5 se aplican los siguientes estándares de los** Estándares estatales comunes de matemáticas: **4.MD.A.1, 4.MD.A.2, 4.MD.A.3, 4.MD.B.4 y todos los de** Prácticas matemáticas.

Measure Length

centimeter (cm)

fluid ounce (fl oz)

cup (c)

foot (ft)

decimeter (dm)

formula

A unit of liquid volume in the customary system.
8 fluid ounces = 1 cup

A unit of measure in the metric system that equals one hundredth of a meter.
100 cm = 1 m

A U.S. customary unit of length equal to 12 inches.

A unit of liquid volume in the customary system that equals 8 fluid ounces.

An equation with letters or symbols that describes a rule.

The formula for the area of a rectangle is:

$A = l \times w$
where A is the area, l is the length, and w is the width.

A unit of measure in the metric system that equals one tenth of a meter.
10 dm = 1 m

gallon (gal)

kilogram (kg)

gram (g)

kiloliter (kL)

inch (in.)

kilometer
(km)

A unit of mass in the metric system that equals one thousand grams.
1 kg = 1,000 g

A unit of liquid volume in the customary system that equals 4 quarts.

A unit of liquid volume in the metric system that equals one thousand liters.
1 kL = 1,000 L

The basic unit of mass in the metric system.

A unit of length in the metric system that equals 1,000 meters.
1 km = 1,000 m

A U.S. customary unit of length.
Example:

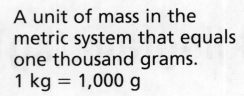

1 inch

length

liter (L)

line plot

mass

liquid volume

meter (m)

The basic unit of liquid volume in the metric system. 1 liter = 1,000 milliliters

The measure of a line segment or the distance across the longer side of a rectangle.

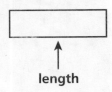

length

The measure of the amount of matter in an object.

A diagram that shows the frequency of data on a number line. Also called a dot plot.

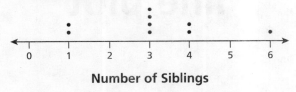

Number of Siblings

The basic unit of length in the metric system.

A measure of the space a liquid occupies.

metric system

milliliter (mL)

mile (mi)

millimeter (mm)

milligram (mg)

ounce (oz)

A unit of liquid volume in the metric system. 1,000 mL = 1 L

A base ten system of measurement.

A unit of length in the metric system. 1,000 mm = 1 m

A U.S. customary unit of length equal to 5,280 feet.

A unit of weight. 16 ounces = 1 pound

A unit of liquid volume (also called a fluid ounce). 8 ounces = 1 cup

A unit of mass in the metric system. 1,000 mg = 1g

perimeter

quart (qt)

pint (pt)

ton

pound (lb)

width

A customary unit of liquid volume that equals 32 ounces or 4 cups.

The distance around a figure.

A unit of weight that equals 2,000 pounds.

A customary unit of liquid volume that equals 16 fluid ounces.

The distance across the shorter side of a rectangle.

width

A unit of weight in the U.S. customary system.

yard (yd)

A U.S. customary unit of length equal to 3 feet.

Name _____

Parts of a Meter

VOCABULARY
millimeter
centimeter
decimeter
meter

Find these units on your meter strip.

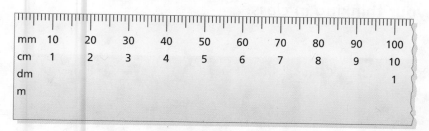

1. Find one **millimeter** (1 mm) on your strip.
   What objects are about 1 mm wide?

   _____

2. Find one **centimeter** (1 cm) on your strip.
   How many millimeters are in 1 cm?

   _____

3. What objects are about 1 centimeter wide?

   _____

4. Find one **decimeter** (1 dm) on your strip.
   How many centimeters are in 1 decimeter?

   _____

   This is one **meter** (1 m) that has been folded into
   decimeters to fit on the page.

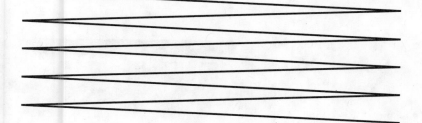

5. How many decimeters are in 1 meter?

   _____

Choose Appropriate Units

Record which metric unit of length is best for measuring each object. Be prepared to justify your thinking in class.

6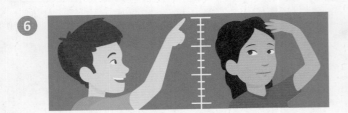

_____

7

_____

8

_____

9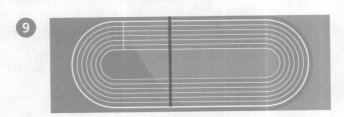

_____

10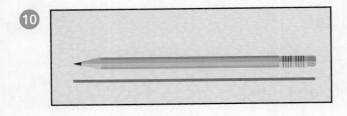

_____

11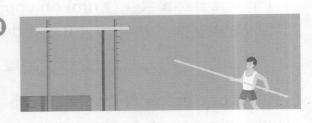

_____

12

_____

13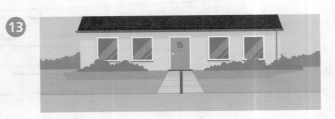

_____

Measure Length

Name _____

Metric Prefixes

VOCABULARY
kilometer
metric system

Units of Length

kilometer	hectometer	dekameter	meter	decimeter	centimeter	millimeter
km	hm	dam	m	dm	cm	mm
10 × 1 hm	10 × 1 dam	10 × 1 m	10 × 1 dm	10 × 1 cm	10 × 1 mm	
1 km = 1,000 m	1 hm = 100 m	1 dam = 10 m		10 dm = 1 m	100 cm = 1 m	1,000 mm = 1 m

14 What words do you know that can help you remember what the prefixes (kilo-, hecto-, deka-, deci-, centi-, milli-) mean in the **metric system**?

_____

_____

_____

15 How do the lengths of the different units relate to each other?

_____

_____

16 How many meters are in 1 **kilometer**? _____

17 How many millimeters are in 1 m? _____

18 How many centimeters are in 1 m? _____

19 What makes the metric system easy to understand?

_____

_____

Convert Metric Units of Measure

You can use a table to convert measurements.

20 How many decimeters are

in one meter? _____

21 Complete the equation.

1 meter = _____ decimeters

Meters	Decimeters
2	2 × 10 = 20
4	__ × 10 = ____
6	6 × _____ = _____
8	_____ = ____

22 Complete the table. Explain how you
found the number of decimeters in 8 meters.

_____

_____

You can also use a number line to convert measurements.

23 Complete the equation. 1 kilometer = _____ meters

24 Label the double number line to show how
kilometers (km) and meters (m) are related.

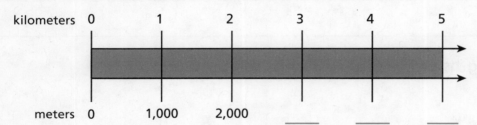

Solve each problem. Label your answers with the correct units.

25 Marsha drove her car 6,835
kilometers last year. How many
meters did Marsha drive last year?

_____

26 John's television is 160 centimeters
wide. How many millimeters wide
is the television?

_____

Solve.

27 5 m = _____ cm   **28** 3 hm = _____ m   **29** 7 km = _____ m

 Check Understanding

Describe the relationship between meters and
kilometers, decimeters, centimeters, and millimeters.

Measure Length

Name _____

Measure Liquid Volume

The base metric unit of **liquid volume** is a **liter**.

Units of Liquid Volume

kiloliter	hectoliter	dekaliter	liter	deciliter	centiliter	milliliter
kL	hL	daL	L	dL	cL	mL
10 × 1 hL	10 × 1 daL	10 × 1 L	10 × 1 dL	10 × 1 cL	10 × 1 mL	
1 kL	1 hL	1 daL		10 dL	100 cL	1,000 mL
= 1,000 L	= 100 L	= 10 L		= 1 L	= 1 L	= 1 L

Ms. Lee cut a two-liter plastic bottle in half to make a one-liter container. She marked the outside to show equal parts.

1 How many **milliliters** of water will fit in the container?

_____

2 How many of these plastic containers will fill a **kiloliter** container? Explain why.

_____

You can use a table or a double number line to convert units of liquid measure.

3 Complete the table.

Liters	Deciliters		
3	3 × 10	= 30	
5	___ × 10	= ___	
7	7 × ___	= ___	
12	_____	= ___	

4 Label the double number line to show how liters (L) and milliliters (mL) are related.

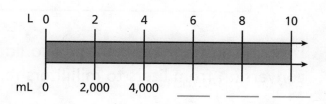

What's the Error?

Dear Math Students,

Today I had to solve this problem.

Meredith wanted to make some punch for a party. The recipe to make the punch called for 3 liters of fruit juice, 2 liters of apple juice, and 1 liter of grape juice. How many milliliters of juice is needed for the recipe? I said that the recipe calls for 600 milliliters of juice. Here is how I solved the problem.

$$3 L + 2 L + 1 L = 6 L \times 100 = 600 \text{ mL}$$

Is my answer correct? If not, please help me understand why it is wrong.

Your friend,
Puzzled Penguin

5 Is Puzzled Penguin correct? Explain your thinking.

_____

_____

6 Use the table to show the conversion from liters to milliliters for each type of juice needed for the recipe.

Liters	Milliliters

7 Describe another way that you could show the conversion from liters to milliliters for each type of juice.

_____

_____

Metric Measures of Liquid Volume and Mass

Name _____

Measure Mass

VOCABULARY
mass
gram
kilogram
milligram

The basic unit of **mass** is a **gram**.

Units of Mass

kilogram	hectogram	dekagram	gram	decigram	centigram	milligram
kg	hg	dag	g	dg	cg	mg
10 × 1 hg	10 × 1 dag	10 × 1 g	10 × 1 dg	10 × 1 cg	10 × 1 mg	
1 kg = 1,000 g	1 hg = 100 g	1 dag = 10 g		10 dg = 1 g	100 cg = 1 g	1,000 mg = 1 g

8 How many **milligrams** are equal to 1 gram? _____

9 How many grams are equal to 1 **kilogram**? _____

If you weighed 1 mL of water, you would find that its mass would be one gram (1 g).

10 Is the gram a small or large unit of measurement? Explain your thinking.

_____

Convert Mass

You can use a table or a double number line to convert units of mass.

11 Complete the table.

Grams	Milligrams
4	4 × 1,000 = 4,000
8	___ × 1,000 = _____
12	12 × ___ = _____
15	_____ = _____

12 Label the double number line to show how kilograms (kg) and grams (g) are related.

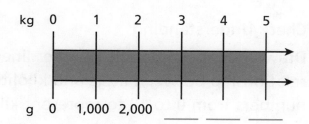

Metric Measures of Liquid Volume and Mass **217**

Practice Converting Metric Units

Solve.

13 Martin measured the mass in grams of four different objects and recorded the information in the table below. Complete the table to find the mass of each object in milligrams.

Grams	Milligrams
4	4,000
7	
11	
15	

14 Olivia bought four different-sized containers and filled them each with water. She recorded the liquid volume of each container in liters below. Complete the table to find the liquid volume of each container in centiliters.

Liters	Centiliters
1	
3	
4	400
6	

15 Hayden has a crayon with a mass of 8 grams. Complete the double number line to find the mass of the crayon in centigrams.

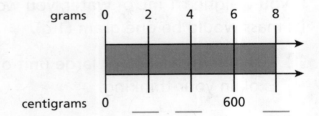

16 Jennifer buys a 2-liter bottle of apple juice and a 3-liter bottle of orange juice at the market. How many deciliters of juice does Jennifer buy in all?

17 Elena has a cat with a mass of 4 kilograms. Ginger's dog has a mass that is 2 times as much as Elena's cat. What is the mass of Ginger's dog in grams?

✓ **Check Understanding**

Draw and label a double number line to show the relationship between liters and kiloliters. Include whole numbers from 0 to 10 to represent kiloliters.

Metric Measures of Liquid Volume and Mass

Name _____

Basic Units of Time

Complete the table.

Units of Time	
① 1 minute = _____ seconds	⑤ 1 year = _____ days
② 1 hour = _____ minutes	⑥ 1 year = _____ weeks
③ 1 day = _____ hours	⑦ 1 year = _____ months
④ 1 week = _____ days	⑧ 1 leap year = _____ days

Convert Units of Time

Complete the table.

⑨

Days	Hours
1	24
2	
3	
4	

⑩

Hours	Minutes
1	60
3	
5	
7	

⑪

Years	Months
3	36
6	
9	
12	

⑫

Hours	Seconds
1	3,600
2	
3	
4	

Solve.

⑬ 36 minutes = _____ seconds

⑭ 41 days = _____ hours

⑮ 72 hours = _____ minutes

⑯ 16 weeks = _____ days

⑰ 6 years = _____ days

⑱ 2 weeks = _____ hours

Make a Line Plot

A **line plot** displays data above a number line. Jamal asked his classmates about the time they spend reading. He organized the data in a table.

19 Use the table to complete the line plot.

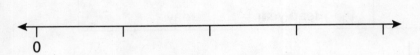

0

Time Spent Reading Each Night (in hours)

Time Spent Reading	Number of Students
0 hours	0
$\frac{1}{4}$ hour	2
$\frac{1}{2}$ hour	5
$\frac{3}{4}$ hour	4
1 hour	4

20 How many classmates did Jamal ask about time spent reading? _____

21 What amount of time had the most responses? _____

Practice

Solve.

22 Fiona asked her friends how much time they spend using a computer at home each night. Use the information in the table at right to make a line plot.

Time Spent on Computer	Number of Students
0 hours	4
$\frac{1}{4}$ hour	4
$\frac{1}{2}$ hour	7
$\frac{3}{4}$ hour	3
1 hour	9

23 Marissa wants to know how many minutes she has practiced the piano. Label the double number line to show how hours and minutes are related. How many minutes has she practiced if she practiced for 4 hours?

_____

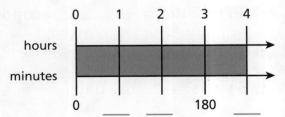

Units of Time

Name _____

Read Elapsed Time

You can imagine clock hands moving to tell how much time has passed.

**How many hours have passed since 12:00 on each clock?
How many minutes?**

24

25

26

_____

_____

**How many hours and how many minutes does the clock show?
Write the time that the clock shows.**

27

28

29

_____ hours

_____ minutes

_____

_____ hours

_____ minutes

_____

_____ hours

_____ minutes

_____

How many hours and minutes have passed between the times shown in:

30 Exercises 27 and 28

31 Exercises 28 and 29

32 Exercises 27 and 29

_____

_____

Solve Elapsed-Time Problems

Solve.

Show your work.

33 The school store is open for 1 hour 45 minutes in the afternoon. The store closes at 2:55 P.M. What time does the school store open?

_____

34 Hannah's practice starts at 9:45 A.M. and ends at 12:35 P.M. How long is Hannah's practice?

_____

35 Bella's dance class starts at 3:05 P.M. and lasts 1 hour 35 minutes. At what time does Bella's dance class end?

_____

36 Lynn went to the mall with her mom. They arrived at the mall at 6:20 P.M. and left at 8:25 P.M. How long were Lynn and her mom at the mall?

_____

37 It takes Reese 32 minutes to walk to school. She gets to school at 7:55 A.M. What time does Reese leave her house to walk to school?

_____

38 Kevin baked a cake. He started making the cake at 8:03 P.M. It took him 1 hour 17 minutes to finish making the cake. What time did Kevin finish making the cake?

_____

✔ **Check Understanding**

Draw a line plot for the following data showing time spent exercising each day and the number of people: 0 hours, 1; $\frac{1}{4}$ hour, 5; $\frac{1}{2}$ hour, 3; $\frac{3}{4}$ hour, 6; 1 hour, 2.

　　　　　　Units of Time

Name _____

Units of Length

VOCABULARY

inch   yard
foot   mile

1 This line segment is 1 **inch** long. Name an object that is about 1 inch long.

_____

2 One **foot** is equal to 12 inches. Name an object that is about 1 foot long.

_____

3 One **yard** is equal to 3 feet or 36 inches. Name an object that is about 1 yard long.

_____

4 Longer distances are measured in miles. One **mile** is equal to 5,280 feet or 1,760 yards. Name a distance that is about 1 mile long.

_____

Convert Customary Units of Length

5 Complete the table.

Feet	Inches
1	12
2	
3	
4	
5	

6 Complete the table.

Yards	Feet
2	6
4	
6	
8	
10	

Solve.

7 9 yards = _____ inches

8 26 feet = _____ inches

9 4 miles = _____ feet

10 2 miles = _____ yards

© Houghton Mifflin Harcourt Publishing Company

Measure Length

Write the measurement of each line segment to the nearest $\frac{1}{8}$ inch.

11

12

13
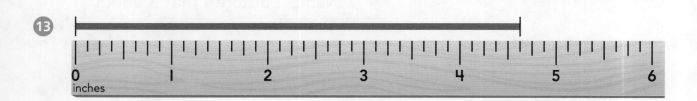

14

15

✓ Check Understanding

Explain how to convert a larger unit of length to a smaller unit of length using customary units. Give an example.

Customary Measures of Length

Pounds and Ounces

VOCABULARY
pound
ounce

The pound is the primary unit of weight in our customary system. One **pound** is equal to 16 **ounces**.

Butter and margarine are sold in 1-pound packages that contain four separately wrapped sticks.

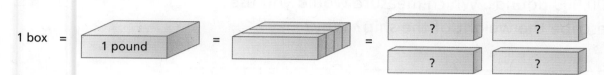

1 box =

1 pound

? ? ? ?

1 What is the weight in ounces of one box?

_____

2 What is the weight in ounces of one stick?

_____

3 Kimba buys a bag of flour that weighs 5 pounds. Complete the table. How many ounces are equal to 5 pounds?

Pounds	Ounces
1	16
2	
3	
4	
5	

_____

4 Describe how to convert pounds to ounces without using a table.

_____

_____

5 When Martin weighed his dog in April, the dog weighed 384 ounces. When he weighed the dog in August, the dog weighed 432 ounces. How many ounces did Martin's dog gain between April and August?

_____

Tons

VOCABULARY
ton

The weight of heavy items such as cars, trucks, boats, elephants, and whales is measured in **tons**. One ton is equal to 2,000 pounds.

6 A ship weighs 12,450 tons. In pounds, the ship weighs 24,900,000 pounds. Which measure would you use to describe the weight of the ship? Why?

_____

_____

_____

7 A trailer can carry 2 tons of cargo. How many pounds of cargo can the trailer carry?

_____

8 One small package weighs 4 ounces. A shipment of small packages weighs a total of 1 ton. How many packages are in the shipment? Show your work.

_____

Practice

Solve.

9 3 tons = _____ pounds

10 7 pounds = _____ ounces

11 5 tons = _____ pounds

12 12 pounds = _____ ounces

13 9 tons = _____ pounds

14 19 pounds = _____ ounces

Name _____

Liquid Volume

In the customary system, the primary unit of liquid volume is a **cup**.

1 cup = 8 **fluid ounces**

2 cups = 1 **pint**

4 cups = 1 **quart**

4 quarts = 1 **gallon**

15 Complete the table.

Quarts	Fluid Ounces
1	32
2	
3	
4	
5	
6	

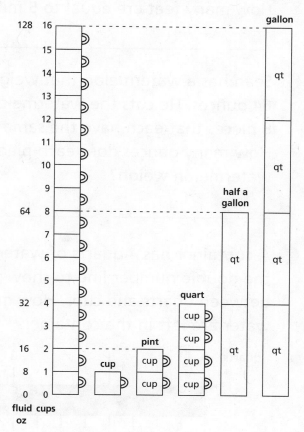

16 Label the double number line to show how gallons (gal) and cups (c) are related.

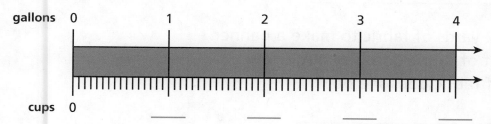

| gallons | 0 | 1 | 2 | 3 | 4 |

cups 0 ____ ____ ____ ____

Solve.

17 3 qt = _____ c

18 10 c = _____ fl oz

19 2 gal = _____ pt

© Houghton Mifflin Harcourt Publishing Company

Solve Real World Problems

Solve.

20 A race is 5 miles long. Complete the table.
How many feet are equal to 5 miles?

_____

Miles	Feet
1	5,280
2	
3	
4	
5	

21 Sean has a watermelon that weighs
64 ounces. He cuts the watermelon into
8 pieces that each have the same weight.
How many ounces does each piece of
watermelon weigh?

Show your work.

_____

22 A container has 4 quarts of water left in it. Complete
the double number line to show the relationship
between quarts and cups. How many cups of
water are left in the container?

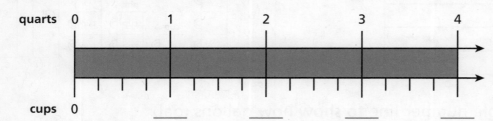

_____

23 Melinda buys 2 yards of fabric to make a banner.
How many feet of fabric does she buy? How
many inches of fabric does she buy?

_____

✓ **Check Understanding**

When converting from a larger unit of measure to a
smaller unit, which operation do you use?

_____

Customary Measures of Weight and Liquid Volume

Solve.

1 9 m = _____ cm

2 5 L = _____ mL

Solve.

Show your work.

3 Brianna started mowing the lawn at 1:40 P.M. She mowed for 55 minutes. At what time did Brianna stop mowing the lawn?

_____

4 Sam cut a 28-foot rope into 4 equal pieces. How long is each piece of rope in inches?

_____

5 Sadie drew a double number line to find the number of fluid ounces in 4 cups. What numbers for fluid ounces will complete the labels?

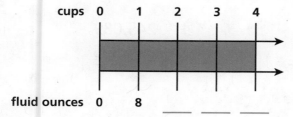

cups   0   1   2   3   4

fluid ounces   0   8   ___ ___ ___

Name _____ Date _____

Add or subtract.

1
$$146$$
$$+\ 313$$

2
$$65{,}783$$
$$+\ 37{,}149$$

3
$$3{,}908$$
$$+\ \ \ 281$$

4
$$751$$
$$-\ 340$$

5
$$18{,}934$$
$$+\ \ 7{,}225$$

6
$$589{,}831$$
$$+\ \ 46{,}230$$

7
$$3{,}792$$
$$+\ 1{,}436$$

8
$$70{,}409$$
$$-\ \ 7{,}382$$

9
$$463$$
$$+\ 572$$

10
$$7{,}833$$
$$-\ 6{,}312$$

11
$$67{,}492$$
$$-\ 28{,}561$$

12
$$417$$
$$-\ 332$$

13
$$954{,}612$$
$$-\ \ 47{,}831$$

14
$$5{,}067$$
$$-\ 3{,}543$$

15
$$245{,}089$$
$$-\ 117{,}395$$

© Houghton Mifflin Harcourt Publishing Company

Name _____

Units of Perimeter

VOCABULARY
perimeter
length
width
formula

The prefix *peri-* means "around." The suffix *-meter* means "measure." **Perimeter** is the measurement of the distance around the outside of a figure.

X

Y

Z

Key:

├────┤ = 1 cm

Length = *l*

Width = *w*

Perimeter = *P*

1 The measurement unit for these rectangles is 1 centimeter (1 cm). How can you find the total number of centimeters around the outside of each rectangle?

_____

_____

2 What is the perimeter of rectangle X? of rectangle Y? of rectangle Z?

_____

_____

3 How did you find the perimeter of each rectangle?

_____

_____

4 Look at the key at the top of the page: **length** is the distance across the longer side of a rectangle and **width** is the distance across the shorter side. Perimeter is the total distance around the outside. Use the letters *l*, *w*, and *P* to write a **formula** for the perimeter of a rectangle.

_____

Units of Area

Area is the total number of square units that cover a figure.
Each square unit inside these rectangles is 1 cm long
and 1 cm wide, so it is 1 square centimeter (1 sq cm).

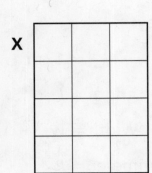

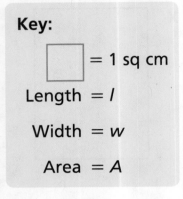

Key:

☐ = 1 sq cm

Length = *l*

Width = *w*

Area = *A*

5 How can you find the total number of square
centimeters inside each rectangle?

_____

_____

6 What is the area of rectangle X? of rectangle Y?
of rectangle Z?

_____

_____

7 Using *l* to stand for length, *w* to stand for width, and
A to stand for area, what formula can you write for
finding the area of any rectangle?

_____

_____

8 Why does the same formula work for all rectangles?

_____

_____

Perimeter and Area of Rectangles

Name _____

Review Perimeter and Area

Perimeter and Area

Perimeter and area are measured with different kinds of units: units of distance or length for perimeter and square units for area.

Perimeter is the total distance around the outside of a figure.

This rectangle has 4 units along its length and 3 units along its width. To find the perimeter, you add the distances of all of the sides:

$$l + w + l + w = P$$

Area is the total number of square units that cover a figure.

For rectangles, area can be seen as an array of squares. This rectangle is an array of 4 squares across (length) and 3 squares down (width). To find its area, you can multiply length times width:

$$l \times w = A$$

Practice with Perimeter and Area

Find the perimeter of rectangle A. Find the area of rectangle B.
1 unit = 1 inch

9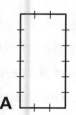

A   B   _____

          _____

10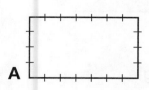

A   B   _____

          _____

Calculate Perimeter and Area

Find the perimeter and area of each rectangle.

11

2 mi [9 mi] _____

12

4 m [4 m] _____

13

5 ft [3 ft] _____

14

4 cm [8 cm] _____

Solve.

15 The area of the rectangle is 60 square meters. One side of the rectangle has a length of 10 meters. What is the unknown side length?

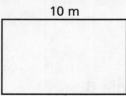

10 m

_____

16 The perimeter of the rectangle is 32 inches. One side of the rectangle has a length of 11 inches. What is the unknown side length?

11 in.

_____

17 The perimeter of a rectangle is 56 mm. Three of the sides have a length of 15 mm, 13 mm, and 15 mm. What is the unknown side length?

_____

18 The area of a rectangle is 81 square inches. One side of the rectangle has a length of 9 inches. What is the unknown side length?

_____

 Check Understanding

Explain how to find the perimeter and area of a rectangle. Give examples as part of your explanation.

© Houghton Mifflin Harcourt Publishing Company

Name _____

Solve Real World Measurement Problems

1 Ethan has a piece of string that is 6 meters long. *Show your work.*
He cuts the string into 3 pieces of equal length.
How many centimeters long is each piece of string?

_____

2 Jamal put a cantaloupe with a mass of 450 grams in
a bag. He adds another cantaloupe that had a mass
of 485 grams. How many grams of cantaloupe are
in the bag?

_____

3 Tanisha has 35 milliliters of lemon juice. She divides
the juice evenly into 5 different containers. How much
juice does she pour into each container?

_____

4 Katherine has some rocks that weigh 4 pounds.
She puts the rocks into 2 groups, each with the same
weight. What is the weight of each group in ounces?

_____

5 Grace buys a yellow ribbon that is 2 feet long and a pink
ribbon that is 8 feet long. How many times as long is the
pink ribbon as the yellow ribbon? How many inches of
ribbon does Grace have in all?

_____

6 Adriana has one gallon of juice. She pours the juice into
containers that each hold one pint of juice. She gives
two pints to her friends. How many pints of juice are left?

_____

7 Jamison ran 1,780 feet yesterday. Today he ran 2,165 feet.
How many yards did Jamison run the past two days?

_____

Solve Real World Measurement Problems (continued)

8 A store sells 89 gallons of milk in May and 82 gallons of milk in June. Altogether, how many gallons of milk did the store sell in May and June?

Show your work.

_____

9 Felix has a dog that weighs 38 pounds. Felix's dog weighs twice as much as Marcell's dog. In ounces, how much more does Felix's dog weigh than Marcell's dog?

_____

10 Grant ran 500 meters around a track. Harry ran 724 meters around the same track. How many more meters did Harry run than Grant?

_____

Perimeter and Area Word Problems

11 The area of the rectangular sandbox is 32 square feet. The short side of the sandbox measures 4 feet. How long is the long side of the sandbox?

_____

12 One wall in Dennis's square bedroom is 13 feet long. What is the perimeter of Dennis's bedroom?

_____

13 A square playground has an area of 900 square feet. What is the length of each side of the playground?

_____

14 A rectangular rug has a perimeter of 20 feet. The length of the rug is 6 feet. What is the width of the rug in inches?

_____

✓ Check Understanding

What formula could you use to solve Problem 12? _____

Solve Measurement Problems

Name

Math and Gardens

Gardens come in all shapes and sizes and can include flowers, vegetables, and many other plants. A Dutch garden is a type of garden that is often a rectangle made up of smaller rectangles and squares, called flowerbeds. A hedge or wall is often placed around the perimeter of the garden. Dutch gardens are known for having very colorful, tightly packed flowers. The Sunken Garden is a famous Dutch garden at Kensington Palace in London, England.

Jared looked up some information about taking care of a garden. He discovered that you need to water and fertilize a garden regularly to help the plants grow. The information he found is shown in the table at the right.

Gardening Information	
Fertilizer	4 ounces per 100 sq feet
Water	30 gallons every 3 days

Use the diagram below to answer the questions. It shows a planned flowerbed for a Dutch garden. The perimeter of the flowerbed is 200 feet.

10 ft [_____ ? _____]

1 What is the length of the unknown side?

Show your work.

_____

2 What is the area of the flowerbed?

_____

3 How many ounces of fertilizer should be used on the flowerbed?

_____

4 How many cups of water are used every 9 days?

_____

Rectangles in Gardens

Padma wants to create a rectangular
shaped garden in her backyard.
She wants to have a total of three
flowerbeds, two of which will be the
same size. She drew a diagram of how
she wants the garden to look. Use the
diagram to answer the questions below.

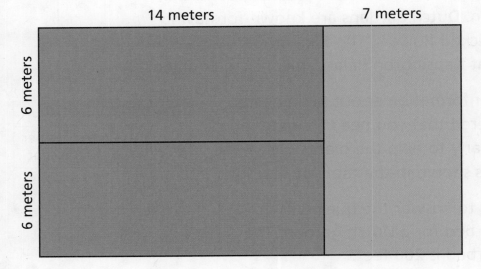

14 meters   7 meters

6 meters

6 meters

5 What is the perimeter of the entire blue section
of flowerbeds?

Show your work.

_____

6 Which section of the garden has a greater perimeter, the
green section or the entire blue section? How much greater?

_____

7 What is the area of the whole garden?

_____

8 Padma decides to plant tulips in one of the blue flowerbeds
and roses in the green flowerbed. Compare the area of the
tulip flowerbed and the rose flowerbed using >, <, or =.

Focus on Mathematical Practices

Solve.

Show your work.

1   The area of a rectangle is 63 square feet. One side of the rectangle has a width of 7 feet. What is the unknown side length?

_____

2   Hayden put 2 cups of lemon juice and 5 times as much water into a jar to make a jar of lemonade. How many fluid ounces of lemonade were in the jar?

_____

3   Jasmine bought a 4-kilogram block of modeling clay. She wants to divide it into 8 equal blocks. What will be the mass of each block in grams?

_____

4   The perimeter of the rectangle is 40 meters. What is the length of one of the long sides?

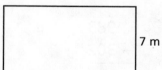
7 m

_____

_____

5   A crew is paving the parking lot shown in the diagram. They will pave it in two stages.

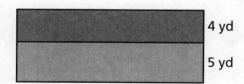
4 yd
5 yd

The total area of the parking lot is 207 square yards. What is the length of one of the long sides of the parking lot?

_____

Add or subtract.

1   17,348
   + 4,419

2   817
   − 736

3   29,713
   − 1,882

4   4,385
   − 2,241

5   9,405
   + 793

6   40,219
   − 34,477

7   384
   + 614

8   4,970
   − 3,548

9   612,498
   − 61,579

10   983
   − 302

11   990,054
   − 247,175

12   32,184
   + 68,472

13   7,569
   + 6,335

14   519,045
   + 453,788

15   578
   + 333

1 A photograph is 8 centimeters wide. After Kari enlarges the photograph, it is 3 times as wide as the original. How wide is the new photograph in millimeters?

_____ millimeters

2 Describe the relationship between these units of time: hours, minutes, and seconds.

3 Complete the table that relates meters and centimeters.

Meters	Centimeters
1	_____
2	_____
3	300
4	_____

4 What is the area of the rectangle?

17 m

5 m

_____ square meters

5 Classify the conversion below as using × 10, × 100, or × 1,000. Write the letter of the conversion in the correct box.

A   kilograms to grams

B   meters to centimeters

C   deciliters to centiliters

D   hectograms to dekagrams

E   liters to milliliters

F   dekameters to decimeters

× 10	× 100	× 1,000

6 Write the length and width of the rectangle. Then write the perimeter. Be sure to choose the correct unit, inches or square inches, for each answer.

13 in.

Length: [ ] [   ]

12 in.

Width: [ ] [   ]

Perimeter: [ ] [   ]

7 For Exercises 7a and 7b, complete the conversion. Then choose the operation and complete the equation to show how you found your answer.

7a. 12 min = [   ] sec

12 | × 60 / ÷ 60 / × 24 / ÷ 24 | = _____

7b. 14 days = [   ] hours

14 | × 60 / ÷ 60 / × 24 / ÷ 24 | = _____

8 For Exercises 8a–8d, choose Yes or No to tell whether the conversion between the metric units is correct.

8a. Divide by 100 to convert kiloliters to dekaliters.   ○ Yes   ○ No

8b. Multiply by 10 to convert milligrams to centigrams.   ○ Yes   ○ No

8c. Divide by 1,000 to convert grams to kilograms.   ○ Yes   ○ No

8d. Divide by 10 to convert kilometers to hectometers.   ○ Yes   ○ No

9 Find the perimeter and area of the rectangle.

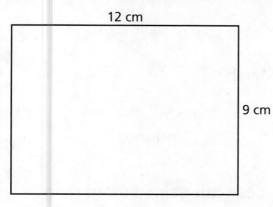

12 cm

9 cm

$P =$ ⬚ centimeters

$A =$ ⬚ square centimeters

10 Draw a line to match equivalent measurements.

48 inches	9 tons	24 cups	18 pounds
●	●	●	●

●	●	●	●
18,000 pounds	288 ounces	4 feet	192 fluid ounces

11 During a speech, a motivational speaker says, "There are 1,440 seconds in each day. How will you spend yours?" Do you agree or disagree with the speaker? Explain your reasoning using words and numbers.

12. A bear cub weighed 64 ounces in March. After three months, it weighed 31 pounds.

Part A

How many pounds did the cub weigh in March?

_____ pounds

Part B

Use words and numbers to show that the bear cub gained more than 25 pounds after three months.

13. Jill asked her classmates how many hours of sleep they got last night. She displayed the data in the line plot shown. How many classmates did Jill ask about the time spent sleeping?

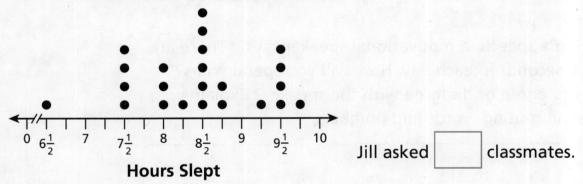

Hours Slept

Jill asked ☐ classmates.

14. Which mass is equivalent to 55 dekagrams? Mark all that apply.

(A) 55 kilograms

(D) 5 hectograms

(B) 550 grams

(E) 550,000 milligrams

(C) 5,500 centigrams

(F) 55,000 decigrams

15 A rectangular scarf has an area of 192 square inches.
The short sides of the scarf are each 6 inches long.

Part A

Use the labels from the list to complete the model.
Labels can be used more than once.

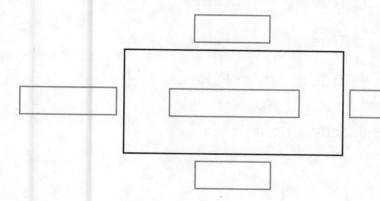

$$l = ?$$
$$w = 6 \text{ in.}$$
$$A = 192 \text{ sq in.}$$

Part B

What is the perimeter of the scarf? Show your work.

16 A rectangular cafeteria tray measures 18 inches on the
long sides. It measures 12 inches on the short sides.
What is the perimeter of the tray?

_____ inches

17 A bag of rice has a mass of 3 kilograms. Jackie buys 17 bags
of rice for the school cafeteria. How many grams of rice did
Jackie buy? Explain how you solved this problem.

18 For Exercises 18a–18e, choose True or False for the conversion.

18a. 8 ft = 96 in.   ○ True   ○ False

18b. 9 lb = 72 oz   ○ True   ○ False

18c. 8 pt = 4 qt   ○ True   ○ False

18d. 3 yd = 36 ft   ○ True   ○ False

18e. 4 gal = 16 pt   ○ True   ○ False

19 A movie starts at 12:45 P.M. and is exactly 1 hour 35 minutes long.

Part A
What time does the movie end?

Part B

It takes Lynn 25 minutes to get to the movie theater. She wants to meet her friends at the theater at least 15 minutes before the movie starts. What is the latest time Lynn can leave her house? Explain how you found your answer.

20 Choose a number from the first column and a unit from the second column to make a measurement that is equivalent to 2 meters.

Number	Unit
○ 100	○ decimeters
○ 20,000	○ centimeters
○ 200	○ millimeters

Patio Design Plans

Gio wants to build a fenced rectangular patio. He has a box of 36 one-foot by one-foot slate tiles.

1 List all the possible rectangular floor designs (length × width) using only whole tiles. Which floor designs do not make sense for this problem? Explain.

_____

_____

_____

_____

2 Find the perimeter for each floor plan. Why do some floor plans have the same perimeter?

_____

_____

_____

3 Gio wants to include a fence around the patio. He needs to keep the cost under $200. He is interested in two kinds of fence. One kind costs $7 per foot and the other costs $9 per foot. Which floor plans could he choose? Identify the least expensive choice.

_____

_____

_____

_____

_____

4 Gio decides to use the floor plan that is 9 feet by 4 feet. He wants
   to put a rectangular table that is 48 inches long and 36 inches
   wide on the patio. Also, on one end of the patio, he wants to
   put a flower box that is 24 inches long and 12 inches wide. How
   much floor area will the table and the flower box cover? How
   much open area will remain for use on the patio? Explain how you
   solved the problem.

   _____

   _____

   _____

   _____

   _____

5 Suppose Gio changes his mind and decides the patio can be a combination
   of rectangular areas, such as an L-shape, instead of a single rectangular
   shape. Draw and label a diagram of the new design. Be sure to use all of
   the tiles. What is the perimeter of the patio you drew?

6 Gio estimates it will take about 15 minutes per tile to lay the 36 tiles.
   How many hours will it take him to build the patio? If he starts at
   9:00 A.M. and takes a one-hour break at 12:00 noon, what time will
   he finish the patio? Show your work.

   _____

   _____

   _____

Dear Family:

Your child has experience with fractions through measurements and in previous grades. Unit 6 of *Math Expressions* builds on this experience. The main goals of this unit are to:

- understand the meaning of fractions.
- compare unit fractions.
- add and subtract fractions and mixed numbers with like denominators.
- multiply a fraction by a whole number.

Your child will use fraction bars and fraction strips to gain a visual and conceptual understanding of fractions as parts of a whole. Later, your child will use these models to add and subtract fractions and to convert between fractions equal to or greater than 1 and mixed numbers.

Examples of Fraction Bar Modeling:

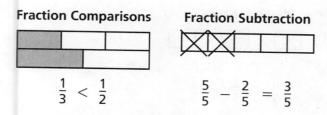

Fraction Comparisons

$$\frac{1}{3} < \frac{1}{2}$$

Fraction Subtraction

$$\frac{5}{5} - \frac{2}{5} = \frac{3}{5}$$

Your child will apply this knowledge about fractions and fraction operations to solve real world problems.

If you have questions or problems, please contact me.

Sincerely,
Your child's teacher

CC SS Unit 6 addresses the following standards from the Common Core State Standards for Mathematics: 4.NF.A.2, 4.NF.B.3, 4.NF.B.3.a, 4.NF.B.3.b, 4.NF.B.3.c, 4.NF.B.3.d, 4.NF.B.4, 4.NF.B.4.a, 4.NF.B.4.b, 4.NF.B.4.c, 4.MD.A.2, 4.MD.B.4, and all Mathematical Practices.

Estimada familia:

Su niño ha usado fracciones al hacer mediciones y en los grados previos. La Unidad 6 de *Math Expressions* amplía esta experiencia. Los objetivos principales de la unidad son:

- comprender el significado de las fracciones.

- comparar fracciones unitarias.

- sumar y restar fracciones y números mixtos con denominadores iguales.

- multiplicar una fracción por un número entero.

Su niño usará barras y tiras de fracciones para comprender y visualizar el concepto de las fracciones como partes de un entero. Luego, usará estos modelos para sumar y restar fracciones y para convertir fracciones igual a o mayor que 1 y números mixtos.

Ejemplos de modelos con barras de fracciones:

Comparaciones de fracciones

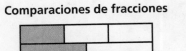

$$\frac{1}{3} < \frac{1}{2}$$

Resta de fracciones

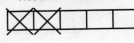

$$\frac{5}{5} - \frac{2}{5} = \frac{3}{5}$$

Su niño aplicará este conocimiento de las fracciones y operaciones con fracciones para resolver problemas cotidianos.

Si tiene alguna duda o algún comentario, por favor comuníquese conmigo.

Atentamente,
El maestro de su niño

CC SS **En la Unidad 6 se aplican los siguientes estándares de los** Estándares estatales comunes de matemáticas: **4.NF.A.2, 4.NF.B.3, 4.NF.B.3.a, 4.NF.B.3.b, 4.NF.B.3.c, 4.NF.B.3.d, 4.NF.B.4, 4.NF.B.4.a, 4.NF.B.4.b, 4.NF.B.4.c, 4.MD.A.2, 4.MD.B.4** **y todos los de** Prácticas matemáticas.

denominator

numerator

fraction

unit fraction

mixed number

The number above the bar in a fraction. It shows the number of equal parts.

Example:

$\frac{3}{4}$ ← numerator $\frac{3}{4} = \frac{1}{4} + \frac{1}{4} + \frac{1}{4}$

The number below the bar in a fraction. It shows the total number of equal parts in the whole.

Example:

$\frac{3}{4}$ ← denominator

A fraction whose numerator is 1. It shows one equal part of a whole.

Example:

$\frac{1}{4}$

A number that is the sum of unit fractions, each an equal part of a set or part of a whole.

Example:

$\frac{3}{4} = \frac{1}{4} + \frac{1}{4} + \frac{1}{4}$

$\frac{5}{4} = \frac{1}{4} + \frac{1}{4} + \frac{1}{4} + \frac{1}{4} + \frac{1}{4}$

A number that can be represented by a whole number and a fraction.

Example:

$4\frac{1}{2} = 4 + \frac{1}{2}$

Name Naomi/Frya

Sums of Fractions

VOCABULARY
unit fraction
fraction
numerator
denominator

A **unit fraction** represents one equal part of a whole. A unit fraction has a numerator of 1. The unit fraction $\frac{1}{d}$ is one of d equal parts.

The fraction bar below is divided into six equal parts, or sixths. Each part is 1 of 6 equal parts, or $\frac{1}{6}$.

| $\frac{1}{6}$ | $\frac{1}{6}$ | $\frac{1}{6}$ | $\frac{1}{6}$ | $\frac{1}{6}$ | $\frac{1}{6}$ |

A **fraction** is the sum of unit fractions. The fraction $\frac{n}{d}$ is the sum of n copies of $\frac{1}{d}$.

numerator → $\frac{n}{d}$ = $\dfrac{\text{number of unit fractions in the fraction}}{\text{number of equal parts in the whole}}$ ← **denominator**

The fraction $\frac{5}{6}$ is the sum of five $\frac{1}{6}$ unit fractions.

$$\frac{5}{6} = \frac{1}{6} + \frac{1}{6} + \frac{1}{6} + \frac{1}{6} + \frac{1}{6} = 5 \times \frac{1}{6}$$

$$\frac{1}{6} + \frac{1}{6} + \frac{1}{6} + \frac{1}{6} + \frac{1}{6} = \frac{5}{6}$$

| $\frac{1}{6}$ | $\frac{1}{6}$ | $\frac{1}{6}$ | $\frac{1}{6}$ | $\frac{1}{6}$ | $\frac{1}{6}$ |

Fold your fraction strips to show each sum of unit fractions. Write the fraction each sum represents.

1. $\frac{1}{3} + \frac{1}{3} =$ 2/3

2. $\frac{1}{8} + \frac{1}{8} + \frac{1}{8} + \frac{1}{8} + \frac{1}{8} =$ 5/8

3. $\frac{1}{4} + \frac{1}{4} =$ 2/4

4. $\frac{1}{6} + \frac{1}{6} + \frac{1}{6} + \frac{1}{6} =$ 4/6

5. $\frac{1}{12} + \frac{1}{12} + \frac{1}{12} + \frac{1}{12} + \frac{1}{12} + \frac{1}{12} =$ 6/12

6. $\frac{1}{12} + \frac{1}{12} + \frac{1}{12} + \frac{1}{12} + \frac{1}{12} + \frac{1}{12} + \frac{1}{12} + \frac{1}{12} =$ 8/12

7. $\frac{1}{8} + \frac{1}{8} + \frac{1}{8} + \frac{1}{8} + \frac{1}{8} + \frac{1}{8} + \frac{1}{8} =$ 7/8

CC SS Content Standards 4.NF.B.3, 4.NF.B.4.a
Mathematical Practices MP2, MP3, MP5, MP6, MP7

Patterns in Fraction Bars

8 Describe at least three patterns you see in the fraction bars below.

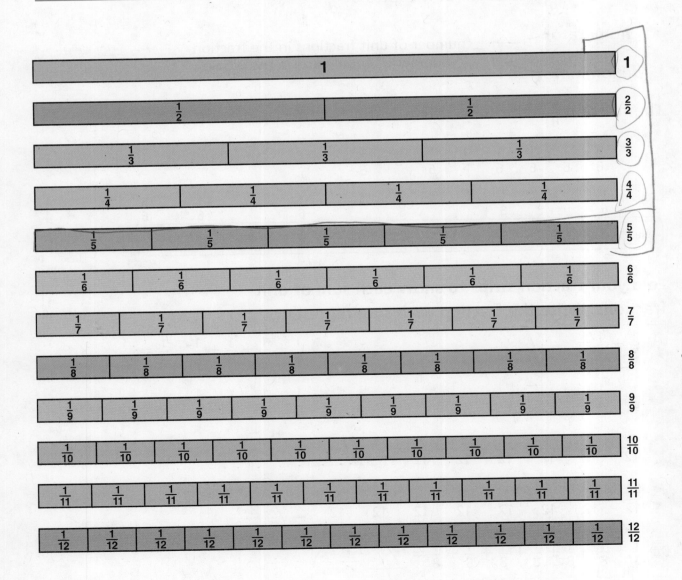

Understand Fractions

Name _____

Sums of Unit Fractions

Shade the fraction bar to show each fraction. Then write the fraction as a sum of unit fractions and as a product of a whole number and a unit fraction. The first one is done for you.

9 $\frac{3}{4} = \underline{\frac{1}{4} + \frac{1}{4} + \frac{1}{4}} = \underline{3 \times \frac{1}{4}}$

$\frac{1}{4}$	$\frac{1}{4}$	$\frac{1}{4}$	$\frac{1}{4}$

10 $\frac{3}{8} = \underline{\frac{1}{8} + \frac{1}{8} + \frac{1}{8}} = \underline{2}$

$\frac{1}{8}$	$\frac{1}{8}$	$\frac{1}{8}$	$\frac{1}{8}$	$\frac{1}{8}$	$\frac{1}{8}$	$\frac{1}{8}$	$\frac{1}{8}$

11 $\frac{5}{5} = \underline{\frac{1}{5} + \frac{1}{5} + \frac{1}{5} + \frac{1}{5} + \frac{1}{5}} = \underline{5 \times \frac{1}{5}}$

$\frac{1}{5}$	$\frac{1}{5}$	$\frac{1}{5}$	$\frac{1}{5}$	$\frac{1}{5}$

12 $\frac{2}{12} = \underline{\hspace{2cm}} = \underline{\hspace{2cm}}$

$\frac{1}{12}$	$\frac{1}{12}$	$\frac{1}{12}$	$\frac{1}{12}$	$\frac{1}{12}$	$\frac{1}{12}$	$\frac{1}{12}$	$\frac{1}{12}$	$\frac{1}{12}$	$\frac{1}{12}$	$\frac{1}{12}$	$\frac{1}{12}$

13 $\frac{4}{7} = \underline{\hspace{3cm}} = \underline{\hspace{2cm}}$

$\frac{1}{7}$	$\frac{1}{7}$	$\frac{1}{7}$	$\frac{1}{7}$	$\frac{1}{7}$	$\frac{1}{7}$	$\frac{1}{7}$

14 $\frac{7}{9} = \underline{\hspace{5cm}} = \underline{\hspace{2cm}}$

$\frac{1}{9}$	$\frac{1}{9}$	$\frac{1}{9}$	$\frac{1}{9}$	$\frac{1}{9}$	$\frac{1}{9}$	$\frac{1}{9}$	$\frac{1}{9}$	$\frac{1}{9}$

Understand Fractions **253**

Fractions as Parts of a Whole

Jon made a large sandwich for the 6 people in his family.
He asked his father to help him cut it into 6 equal pieces.
To do this, they made a paper cutting guide that is as long
as the sandwich. Jon folded the paper into 6 equal parts,
and his father used it to cut the sandwich into equal pieces.

Solve.

Show your work.

15 If each person ate 1 piece of the sandwich, what
fraction of the sandwich did each person eat?
Fold your 6-part fraction strip to show the fraction
of the whole sandwich that each person ate.

_____

16 How many pieces of the whole sandwich did Jon's
mother and father eat altogether? Fold your fraction
strip to show the fraction of the whole sandwich Jon's
mother and father ate in all.

_____

17 After Jon's mother and father got their pieces, what
fraction of the sandwich was left?

_____

18 Jon and his sisters were each able to have one of the
remaining pieces of the sandwich. How many sisters
does Jon have?

_____

✓**Check Understanding**
Explain what a unit fraction is and how unit
fractions are used to build other fractions.

Understand Fractions

Name _____

Fifths that Add to One

Every afternoon, student volunteers help the school librarian put returned books back on the shelves. The librarian puts the books in equal piles on a cart.

One day, Jean and Maria found 5 equal piles on the return cart. They knew there were different ways they could share the job of reshelving the books. They drew fraction bars to help them find all the possibilities.

1 On each fifths bar, circle two groups of fifths to show one way Jean and Maria could share the work. (Each bar should show a different possibility.) Then complete the equation next to each bar to show their shares.

| 1 whole = all of the books |

1 whole   Jean's   Maria's
            share   share

| $\frac{1}{5}$ | $\frac{1}{5}$ | $\frac{1}{5}$ | $\frac{1}{5}$ | $\frac{1}{5}$ |

$\frac{5}{5} = \frac{3}{5} + \frac{2}{5}$

| $\frac{1}{5}$ | $\frac{1}{5}$ | $\frac{1}{5}$ | $\frac{1}{5}$ | $\frac{1}{5}$ |

$\frac{5}{5} = \frac{4}{5} + \frac{1}{5}$

| $\frac{1}{5}$ | $\frac{1}{5}$ | $\frac{1}{5}$ | $\frac{1}{5}$ | $\frac{1}{5}$ |

$\frac{5}{5} = \frac{1}{5} + \frac{4}{5}$

| $\frac{1}{5}$ | $\frac{1}{5}$ | $\frac{1}{5}$ | $\frac{1}{5}$ | $\frac{1}{5}$ |

$\frac{5}{5} = \frac{2}{5} + \frac{3}{5}$

CC SS Content Standards 4.NF.A.2, 4.NF.B.3.a, 4.NF.B.3.b
Mathematical Practices MP2, MP3, MP6, MP8

Sixths that Add to One

The librarian put 6 equal piles of returned books on the cart for Liu and Henry to reshelve. They also drew fraction bars.

2 On each sixths bar, circle two groups of sixths to show one way that Liu and Henry could share the work. (Each bar should show a different possibility.) Then complete the equation next to each bar to show their shares.

1 whole	Liu's share	Henry's share

| $\frac{1}{6}$ | $\frac{1}{6}$ | $\frac{1}{6}$ | $\frac{1}{6}$ | $\frac{1}{6}$ | $\frac{1}{6}$ |

$\frac{6}{6} = \frac{}{6} + \frac{}{6}$

| $\frac{1}{6}$ | $\frac{1}{6}$ | $\frac{1}{6}$ | $\frac{1}{6}$ | $\frac{1}{6}$ | $\frac{1}{6}$ |

$\frac{6}{6} = \frac{}{6} + \frac{}{6}$

| $\frac{1}{6}$ | $\frac{1}{6}$ | $\frac{1}{6}$ | $\frac{1}{6}$ | $\frac{1}{6}$ | $\frac{1}{6}$ |

$\frac{6}{6} = \frac{}{6} + \frac{}{6}$

| $\frac{1}{6}$ | $\frac{1}{6}$ | $\frac{1}{6}$ | $\frac{1}{6}$ | $\frac{1}{6}$ | $\frac{1}{6}$ |

$\frac{6}{6} = \frac{}{6} + \frac{}{6}$

| $\frac{1}{6}$ | $\frac{1}{6}$ | $\frac{1}{6}$ | $\frac{1}{6}$ | $\frac{1}{6}$ | $\frac{1}{6}$ |

$\frac{6}{6} = \frac{}{6} + \frac{}{6}$

Find the Unknown Addend

Write the fraction that will complete each equation.

3 $1 = \frac{7}{7} = \frac{1}{7} +$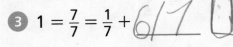

4 $1 = \frac{4}{4} = \frac{3}{4} +$ 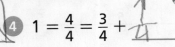 $\frac{1}{4}$

5 $1 = \frac{8}{8} = \frac{3}{8} +$ 5/8

6 $1 = \frac{5}{5} = \frac{2}{5} +$ 3/5

7 $1 = \frac{3}{3} = \frac{2}{3} +$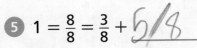

8 $1 = \frac{10}{10} = \frac{6}{10} +$ _____

9 $1 = \frac{6}{6} = \frac{2}{6} +$ _____

10 $1 = \frac{8}{8} = \frac{5}{8} +$ _____

Fractions that Add to One

Name _____

Discuss and Compare Unit Fractions

Use these fraction bars to help you compare the unit fractions. Write > or <.

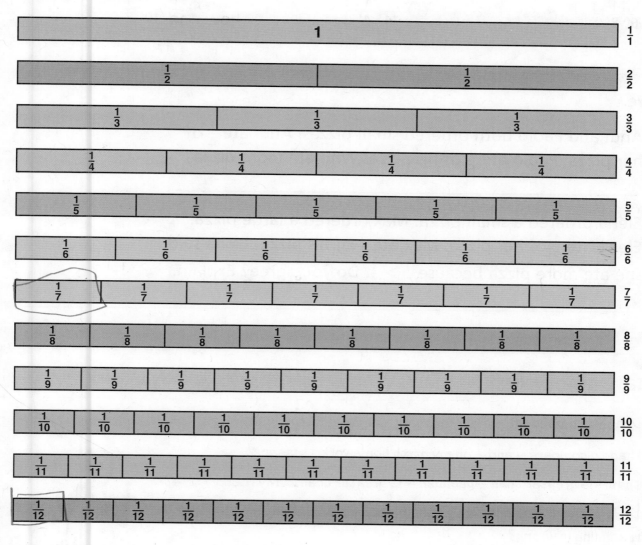

11. $\frac{1}{6}$ ⬡ $\frac{1}{8}$

12. $\frac{1}{5}$ ⬡ $\frac{1}{3}$

13. $\frac{1}{10}$ ⊘ $\frac{1}{12}$

14. $\frac{1}{7}$ ⬡ $\frac{1}{4}$

15. $\frac{1}{9}$ ⬡ $\frac{1}{12}$

16. $\frac{1}{9}$ ⊘ $\frac{1}{11}$

17. Complete this statement:

When comparing two unit fractions, the fraction

with the smaller denominator is  bigg er .

Compare and Order Unit Fractions

Write the unit fractions in order from least to greatest.

18 $\frac{1}{6}$, $\frac{1}{8}$, $\frac{1}{5}$

19 $\frac{1}{11}$, $\frac{1}{4}$, $\frac{1}{8}$

20 $\frac{1}{3}$, $\frac{1}{10}$, $\frac{1}{7}$

_____   _____   _____

Solve.

21 Andi and Paolo both ordered small pizzas. Andi ate $\frac{1}{4}$ of her pizza. Paolo ate $\frac{1}{6}$ of his pizza. Who ate more pizza?

_____

22 Elena ordered a small pizza. Max ordered a large pizza. Elena ate $\frac{1}{3}$ of her pizza. Max ate $\frac{1}{4}$ of his pizza. Elena said she ate more pizza because $\frac{1}{3} > \frac{1}{4}$. Do you agree? Explain.

_____

_____

What's the Error?

Dear Math Students,

I had to compare $\frac{1}{4}$ and $\frac{1}{2}$ on my math homework. I reasoned that $\frac{1}{4}$ is greater than $\frac{1}{2}$ because 4 is greater than 2. My friend told me this isn't right. Can you help me understand why my reasoning is wrong?

Your friend,
Puzzled Penguin

23 Write a response to Puzzled Penguin.

_____

_____

 Check Understanding

Explain how to find pairs of fractions that have a sum of $\frac{5}{5}$.

Fractions that Add to One

Name_____

Add Fractions

The circled parts of this fraction bar show an addition problem.

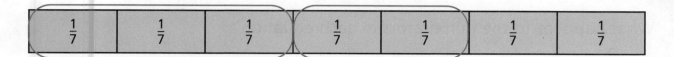

1 Complete this addition equation to match the problem above.

$$\frac{}{7} + \frac{}{7} = \frac{+}{7} = \frac{}{7}$$

Write the numerators to complete each addition equation.

2 $\frac{3}{9} + \frac{4}{9} = \frac{+}{9} = \frac{}{9}$ **3** $\frac{1}{5} + \frac{3}{5} = \frac{+}{5} = \frac{}{5}$ **4** $\frac{2}{8} + \frac{5}{8} = \frac{+}{8} = \frac{}{8}$

5 What happens to the numerators in each equation?

_____

6 What happens to the denominators in each equation?

_____

Subtract Fractions

The circled and crossed-out parts of this fraction bar show a subtraction problem.

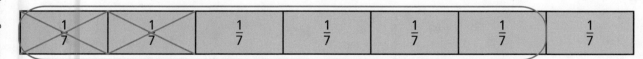

7 Write the numerators to complete the subtraction equation.

$$\frac{}{7} - \frac{}{7} = \frac{-}{7} = \frac{}{7}$$

CC SS Content Standards 4.NF.B.3.a, 4.NF.B.3.d, 4.MD.A.2
Mathematical Practices MP2, MP3, MP4, MP6

Subtract Fractions (continued)

Write the numerators to complete each subtraction equation.

8 $\dfrac{5}{6} - \dfrac{4}{6} = \dfrac{-}{6} = \dfrac{}{6}$ **9** $\dfrac{9}{10} - \dfrac{5}{10} = \dfrac{-}{10} = \dfrac{}{}$ **10** $\dfrac{14}{16} - \dfrac{9}{16} = \dfrac{-}{16} = \dfrac{}{}$

11 What happens to the numerators in each equation?

_____

12 How is subtracting fractions with like denominators similar to adding fractions with like denominators?

_____

_____

Mixed Practice with Addition and Subtraction

Solve each problem. Include the "circled" step in Exercises 16–21.

13 $\dfrac{1}{4} + \dfrac{2}{4} = \boxed{\dfrac{+}{4}} =$ **14** $\dfrac{3}{9} + \dfrac{5}{9} = \boxed{\dfrac{+}{9}} =$ **15** $\dfrac{6}{6} - \dfrac{2}{6} = \boxed{\dfrac{-}{6}} =$

16 $\dfrac{4}{10} + \dfrac{5}{10} =$ **17** $\dfrac{2}{5} + \dfrac{4}{5} =$ **18** $\dfrac{8}{12} - \dfrac{3}{12} =$

19 $\dfrac{5}{7} + \dfrac{2}{7} =$ **20** $\dfrac{7}{11} - \dfrac{4}{11} =$ **21** $\dfrac{8}{8} - \dfrac{5}{8} =$

Solve.

22 $\begin{array}{r} \dfrac{7}{9} \\ - \dfrac{5}{9} \\ \hline \end{array}$ **23** $\begin{array}{r} \dfrac{4}{5} \\ - \dfrac{3}{5} \\ \hline \end{array}$ **24** $\begin{array}{r} \dfrac{1}{3} \\ + \dfrac{2}{3} \\ \hline \end{array}$

25 $\begin{array}{r} \dfrac{2}{11} \\ + \dfrac{7}{11} \\ \hline \end{array}$ **26** $\begin{array}{r} \dfrac{5}{6} \\ - \dfrac{1}{6} \\ \hline \end{array}$ **27** $\begin{array}{r} \dfrac{1}{8} \\ + \dfrac{1}{8} \\ \hline \end{array}$

Add and Subtract Fractions with Like Denominators

Name

Fraction Bars

one whole		$\frac{1}{1}$

| $\frac{1}{2}$ | $\frac{1}{2}$ | $\frac{2}{2}$ |

| $\frac{1}{3}$ | $\frac{1}{3}$ | $\frac{1}{3}$ | $\frac{3}{3}$ |

| $\frac{1}{4}$ | $\frac{1}{4}$ | $\frac{1}{4}$ | $\frac{1}{4}$ | $\frac{4}{4}$ |

| $\frac{1}{5}$ | $\frac{1}{5}$ | $\frac{1}{5}$ | $\frac{1}{5}$ | $\frac{1}{5}$ | $\frac{5}{5}$ |

| $\frac{1}{6}$ | $\frac{1}{6}$ | $\frac{1}{6}$ | $\frac{1}{6}$ | $\frac{1}{6}$ | $\frac{1}{6}$ | $\frac{6}{6}$ |

| $\frac{1}{7}$ | $\frac{1}{7}$ | $\frac{1}{7}$ | $\frac{1}{7}$ | $\frac{1}{7}$ | $\frac{1}{7}$ | $\frac{1}{7}$ | $\frac{7}{7}$ |

| $\frac{1}{8}$ | $\frac{1}{8}$ | $\frac{1}{8}$ | $\frac{1}{8}$ | $\frac{1}{8}$ | $\frac{1}{8}$ | $\frac{1}{8}$ | $\frac{1}{8}$ | $\frac{8}{8}$ |

| $\frac{1}{9}$ | $\frac{1}{9}$ | $\frac{1}{9}$ | $\frac{1}{9}$ | $\frac{1}{9}$ | $\frac{1}{9}$ | $\frac{1}{9}$ | $\frac{1}{9}$ | $\frac{1}{9}$ | $\frac{9}{9}$ |

| $\frac{1}{10}$ | $\frac{1}{10}$ | $\frac{1}{10}$ | $\frac{1}{10}$ | $\frac{1}{10}$ | $\frac{1}{10}$ | $\frac{1}{10}$ | $\frac{1}{10}$ | $\frac{1}{10}$ | $\frac{1}{10}$ | $\frac{10}{10}$ |

| $\frac{1}{12}$ | $\frac{1}{12}$ | $\frac{1}{12}$ | $\frac{1}{12}$ | $\frac{1}{12}$ | $\frac{1}{12}$ | $\frac{1}{12}$ | $\frac{1}{12}$ | $\frac{1}{12}$ | $\frac{1}{12}$ | $\frac{1}{12}$ | $\frac{1}{12}$ | $\frac{12}{12}$ |

Add and Subtract Fractions with Like Denominators **260A**

Add and Subtract Fractions with Like Denominators

Name _____

What's the Error?

Dear Math Students,

My friend said, "If you catch 3 fish and then 2 more fish, how many fish will you have?"
Of course, I know I will have 5 fish! She said, "This is the same problem, but you have fifths instead of fish!"

Can you help me understand what my friend meant and help me find the right answer?

Your friend,
Puzzled Penguin

$$\frac{3}{5} + \frac{2}{5} = \frac{5}{10}$$

28 Write a response to Puzzled Penguin.

_____

_____

_____

Dear Math Students,

My friend said my answer for this problem is wrong too.

She said, "Think about fish again. If you have 4 fish and then eat 3, how many will you have?" What does she mean? What should the answer be?

Your friend,
Puzzled Penguin

$$\frac{4}{5} - \frac{3}{5} = \frac{1}{0}$$

29 Write a response to Puzzled Penguin.

_____

_____

_____

Real World Problems

Draw a model. Then solve.

30 Wayne had $\frac{7}{8}$ cup of trail mix. He ate $\frac{3}{8}$ cup as he was hiking. How many cups does he have now?

_____

31 Reese had $\frac{2}{4}$ cup of orange juice. She added pineapple juice to make a total of $\frac{3}{4}$ cup of juice. How much pineapple juice did she add?

_____

Write an equation. Then solve.

Show your work.

32 Nasira walks $\frac{4}{5}$ mile to school each day. This is $\frac{2}{5}$ mile farther than Kat walks. How far does Kat walk to school?

_____

33 A puppy is now 5 weeks old. It has gained $\frac{8}{16}$ pound since it was born. The puppy weighs $\frac{11}{16}$ pound now. How much did the puppy weigh when it was born?

_____

34 The water in a tub was $\frac{7}{12}$ foot deep. Then Dom added water until it was $\frac{4}{12}$ foot deeper. How deep is the water now?

_____

✓ **Check Understanding**

Circle the correct answer that completes the sentence.
When you add or subtract fractions with like denominators,
the unit _does/does not_ change.

Add and Subtract Fractions with Like Denominators

Complete.

1 $\frac{5}{5} = \frac{1}{5} + $ _____

2 $\frac{6}{6} = \frac{2}{6} + $ _____

3 Write the fraction as a sum of unit fractions and as a product of a whole number and a unit fraction.

$\frac{7}{8} = $ _____ $ = $ _____

Solve.

4 $\frac{3}{5} + \frac{1}{5} = $ _____

5 $\frac{7}{8} - \frac{2}{8} = $ _____

Name _____ Date _____

Add or subtract.

1
```
  246
+ 313
```

2
```
  487
- 378
```

3
```
  5,824
+ 1,355
```

4
```
  7,896
- 5,472
```

5
```
  36,752
+ 15,417
```

6
```
  56,008
-  7,124
```

7
```
  3,726
+ 4,469
```

8
```
  8,034
- 7,311
```

9
```
  438
+ 621
```

10
```
  765
- 334
```

11
```
  45,389
- 28,685
```

12
```
  51,386
+  9,342
```

13
```
  872,385
-  49,817
```

14
```
  428,595
+ 325,957
```

15
```
  506,729
- 388,214
```

Name _____

Mixed Numbers in the Real World

VOCABULARY
mixed number

A **mixed number** is a number that consists of a whole number and a fraction.

$1\frac{4}{6}$ $3\frac{4}{5}$

A fraction greater than 1 has a numerator greater than its denominator.

$\frac{10}{6}$ $\frac{19}{5}$

Mellie's Deli makes sandwiches. This is the price list.

Mellie's Deli

Regular (serves 2).......................... $3.00
Friendship (serves 4)...................... $5.00
Super (serves 10).......................... $12.00
Magna (serves 18).......................... $20.00

Nineteen friends decide to buy lunch for their camping trip. They order two Super sandwiches. Each camper eats 1 serving.

$\frac{10}{10}$
$\frac{9}{6}$

Solve.

1 How many campers does one Super sandwich serve?

10 Campers

2 What fraction of the second sandwich is needed to serve the rest of the campers?

9/10   19 − 10 = 9

3 What fraction of the second sandwich is left over?

$1\frac{9}{10} = \frac{10}{10} = \frac{9}{10} = \frac{1}{10}$

4 What number tells how many Super sandwiches the campers ate in all?

19/10 = $1\frac{9}{10}$

Convert Between Mixed Numbers and Fractions Greater Than 1

Change each mixed number to a fraction and each fraction to a mixed number.

5 $5\frac{2}{3} = \frac{17}{3}$

$3 \times 5 = 15 + 2 = 17$

6 $3\frac{3}{7} = \frac{24}{7}$

$7 \times 3 = 21 + 3 = 24$

7 $6\frac{6}{10} = \frac{66}{10}$

$6 \times 10 = 60 + 6 = 66$

8 $9\frac{1}{4} = \underline{}$

4×4

9 $2\frac{7}{8} = \underline{}$

10 $4\frac{5}{9} = \underline{}$

11 $8\frac{3}{5} = \underline{}$

12 $7\frac{4}{6} = \underline{}$

13 $\frac{40}{6} = 6\frac{4}{6}$

14 $\frac{11}{2} = 5\frac{1}{2}$

$2\overline{)11} \atop \,\underline{-10} \atop 1$ (with 5 above)

15 $\frac{23}{7} = 3\frac{2}{7}$

$7\overline{)23} \atop \underline{-21} \atop 2$ (with 3 above)

16 $\frac{28}{3} = \underline{}$

17 $\frac{22}{4} = \underline{}$

18 $\frac{25}{8} = \underline{}$

19 $\frac{29}{7} = \underline{}$

20 $6\frac{4}{8} = \underline{}$

21 $4\frac{6}{9} = \underline{}$

22 $\frac{16}{3} = \underline{}$

✔ **Check Understanding**

Draw a picture to represent the mixed number for Exercise 17.

Mixed Numbers and Fractions Greater Than 1

Name _____

Understand Fractions Greater Than 1 and Mixed Numbers

1 whole

$\frac{1}{8}$	$\frac{1}{8}$	$\frac{1}{8}$	$\frac{1}{8}$	$\frac{1}{8}$	$\frac{1}{8}$	$\frac{1}{8}$	$\frac{1}{8}$
$\frac{1}{8}$	$\frac{1}{8}$	$\frac{1}{8}$	$\frac{1}{8}$	$\frac{1}{8}$	$\frac{1}{8}$	$\frac{1}{8}$	$\frac{1}{8}$
$\frac{1}{8}$	$\frac{1}{8}$	$\frac{1}{8}$	$\frac{1}{8}$	$\frac{1}{8}$	$\frac{1}{8}$	$\frac{1}{8}$	$\frac{1}{8}$
$\frac{1}{8}$	$\frac{1}{8}$	$\frac{1}{8}$	$\frac{1}{8}$	$\frac{1}{8}$	$\frac{1}{8}$	$\frac{1}{8}$	$\frac{1}{8}$
$\frac{1}{8}$	$\frac{1}{8}$	$\frac{1}{8}$	$\frac{1}{8}$	$\frac{1}{8}$	$\frac{1}{8}$	$\frac{1}{8}$	$\frac{1}{8}$
$\frac{1}{8}$	$\frac{1}{8}$	$\frac{1}{8}$	$\frac{1}{8}$	$\frac{1}{8}$	$\frac{1}{8}$	$\frac{1}{8}$	$\frac{1}{8}$
$\frac{1}{8}$	$\frac{1}{8}$	$\frac{1}{8}$	$\frac{1}{8}$	$\frac{1}{8}$	$\frac{1}{8}$	$\frac{1}{8}$	$\frac{1}{8}$

$\frac{1}{5}$	$\frac{1}{5}$	$\frac{1}{5}$	$\frac{1}{5}$	$\frac{1}{5}$
$\frac{1}{5}$	$\frac{1}{5}$	$\frac{1}{5}$	$\frac{1}{5}$	$\frac{1}{5}$
$\frac{1}{5}$	$\frac{1}{5}$	$\frac{1}{5}$	$\frac{1}{5}$	$\frac{1}{5}$
$\frac{1}{5}$	$\frac{1}{5}$	$\frac{1}{5}$	$\frac{1}{5}$	$\frac{1}{5}$
$\frac{1}{5}$	$\frac{1}{5}$	$\frac{1}{5}$	$\frac{1}{5}$	$\frac{1}{5}$
$\frac{1}{5}$	$\frac{1}{5}$	$\frac{1}{5}$	$\frac{1}{5}$	$\frac{1}{5}$
$\frac{1}{5}$	$\frac{1}{5}$	$\frac{1}{5}$	$\frac{1}{5}$	$\frac{1}{5}$

Understand Fractions Greater Than 1 and Mixed Numbers (continued)

1 whole

1 whole
1 whole
1 whole
1 whole
1 whole
1 whole
1 whole

1 whole
1 whole
1 whole
1 whole
1 whole
1 whole
1 whole

Mixed Numbers and Fractions Greater Than 1

Name _____

Practice Addition and Subtraction with Fractions Greater Than 1

Add or subtract.

1 $\frac{8}{5} + \frac{3}{5} =$ _$\frac{11}{5}$_

2 $\frac{6}{9} + \frac{12}{9} =$ _$\frac{18}{9}$_

3 $\frac{10}{7} - \frac{3}{7} =$ _$\frac{7}{7} = 1$_

4 $\frac{10}{8} + \frac{7}{8} =$ _$\frac{17}{9}$_

5 $\frac{9}{6} - \frac{4}{6} =$ _$\frac{5}{6}$_

6 $\frac{19}{10} - \frac{7}{10} =$ _$\frac{12}{10}$_

Add Mixed Numbers with Like Denominators

Add.

7
$$2\frac{3}{5}$$
$$+ 1\frac{1}{5}$$
$$3\frac{4}{5}$$

8
$$1\frac{2}{5}$$
$$+ 3\frac{4}{5}$$
$$5\frac{6}{5} \quad 5\frac{1}{5}$$

9
$$3\frac{5}{8}$$
$$+ 1\frac{3}{8} = 1$$
$$5$$

10
$$5\frac{2}{3}$$
$$+ 2\frac{2}{3}$$
$$8 \quad \frac{1}{3}$$

Subtract Mixed Numbers with Like Denominators

Subtract.

11
$$5\frac{6}{8}$$
$$- 3\frac{3}{8}$$
$$2\frac{3}{8}$$

12
$$5\frac{2}{8}$$
$$- 4\frac{5}{8}$$
$$1\frac{5}{8}$$

13
$$3\frac{1}{5}$$
$$- 1\frac{3}{5}$$
$$2\frac{3}{5}$$

14
$$5\frac{1}{6}$$
$$- 3\frac{4}{6}$$

Explain each solution.

15
$$5 \quad ^{7 + 2 = 9}$$
$$6\frac{2}{7} = 5\frac{9}{7}$$
$$- 1\frac{5}{7} = 1\frac{5}{7}$$
$$4\frac{4}{7}$$

16
$$5 \quad ^{6 + 2 = 8}$$
$$6\frac{2}{6} = 5\frac{8}{6}$$
$$- 1\frac{5}{6} = 1\frac{5}{6}$$
$$4\frac{3}{6}$$

17
$$5 \quad ^{11 + 2 = 13}$$
$$6\frac{2}{11} = 5\frac{13}{11}$$
$$- 1\frac{5}{11} = 1\frac{5}{11}$$
$$4\frac{8}{11}$$

What's the Error?

Dear Math Students,

Here is a subtraction problem that I tried to solve.

Is my answer correct? If not, please help
me understand why it is wrong.

Your friend,
Puzzled Penguin

$$7\frac{3}{8}$$
$$-1\frac{5}{8}$$
$$\overline{6\frac{2}{8}}$$

18 Write a response to Puzzled Penguin.

_____

_____

_____

_____

Compare and Subtract

**Compare each pair of mixed numbers using > or <. Then subtract
the lesser mixed number from the greater mixed number.**

19 $3\frac{2}{5}$; $1\frac{4}{5}$ _____

20 $1\frac{8}{9}$; $2\frac{2}{9}$ _____

21 $1\frac{3}{11}$; $1\frac{6}{11}$ _____

22 $4\frac{1}{8}$; $2\frac{7}{8}$ _____

23 $3\frac{2}{6}$; $4\frac{3}{6}$ _____

24 $10\frac{1}{3}$; $7\frac{2}{3}$ _____

✔ **Check Understanding**

Represent your solution to Exercise 22 by drawing fraction bars.

Add and Subtract Mixed Numbers with Like Denominators

Name Naomi ~~[scribbled]~~

Practice with Fractions and Mixed Numbers

Write the fraction that will complete each equation.

1 $1 = \frac{4}{4} = \frac{1}{4} + $ _3/4_   **2** $1 = \frac{10}{10} = \frac{9}{10} + $ _$\frac{1}{10}$_   **3** $1 = \frac{8}{8} = \frac{4}{8} + $ _$\frac{4}{8}$_

Write each fraction as a sum of fractions in two different ways.

4 $\frac{5}{6}$ _$\frac{1}{6} + \frac{4}{6} + \frac{3}{6} + \frac{2}{6}$_

5 $\frac{8}{10}$ _$\frac{1}{10} + \frac{1}{10}, \frac{4}{10} + \frac{4}{10}$_

6 $\frac{6}{8}$ _$\frac{3}{8} + \frac{3}{8}, \frac{4}{8} + \frac{2}{8}$_

7 $\frac{10}{6}$ _$\frac{5}{6} + \frac{5}{6}, \frac{4}{6} + \frac{1}{6}$_

Write each fraction as a mixed number.

8 $\frac{11}{8} = $ _$1\frac{3}{8}$_ $8\overline{)11}$ -8 3

9 $\frac{15}{6} = $ _$2\frac{3}{6}$_ $6\overline{)15}$ -12

10 $\frac{32}{5} = $ _$6\frac{2}{5}$_ $5\overline{)32}$ -30 2

Write each mixed number as a fraction.

11 $3\frac{2}{5} = $ _$\frac{17}{5}$_

12 $1\frac{1}{4} = $ _$\frac{5}{4}$_ $4 \times 1 = 4 \frac{3}{?}$

13 $2\frac{11}{12} = $ _$\frac{35}{12}$_ $\frac{35}{}$

$5 \times 3 = 15 + 2 = \boxed{17}$ $+1=5$ $12 \times 2 = 24 + 11$ 35

Add or subtract.

14 $\frac{2}{5} + \frac{1}{5} = $ _$\frac{3}{5}$_

15 $\frac{3}{9} + \frac{6}{9} = $ _$\frac{9}{9} = 1$_

16 $\frac{4}{6} - \frac{3}{6} = $ _$\frac{1}{6}$_

17 $\frac{5}{7} - \frac{2}{7} = $ _$\frac{3}{7}$_

18 $\frac{7}{12} + \frac{1}{12} = $ _$\frac{8}{12}$_

19 $\frac{10}{10} - \frac{4}{10} = $ _$\frac{6}{10}$_

20 $\frac{9}{4} + \frac{5}{4} = $ _$\frac{14}{4}$_

21 $\frac{23}{8} - \frac{12}{8} = $ _$\frac{11}{8}$_ 35

22 $\frac{5}{2} + \frac{3}{2} = $ _$\frac{8}{2}$_

CC SS Content Standards 4.NF.B.3.a, 4.NF.B.3.b, 4.NF.B.3.c, 4.NF.B.3.d, 4.MD.A.2, 4.MD.B.4 Mathematical Practices MP1, MP3, MP4, MP6

Practice with Fractions and Mixed Numbers **269**

Practice with Fractions and Mixed Numbers (continued)

Add or subtract.

23 $3\frac{1}{4}$
  $+ 5\frac{2}{4}$

$8\frac{3}{4}$

24 $4\frac{6}{8}$
  $- 3\frac{3}{8}$

$\frac{6}{8} - \frac{3}{6}$ $\frac{3}{8}$

25 $\overset{+1}{1}\frac{3}{5}$
  $+ 1\frac{2}{5}$

$\frac{5}{3} = 1$ 3

26 $4\frac{1}{3}$ 3
  $- 1\frac{2}{3}$

$2\frac{2}{3}$

27 $2\frac{5}{10}$
  $+ 4\frac{9}{10}$

$7\frac{4}{10}$

28 $4\,10\frac{5}{8}$ $+ \frac{2}{8} =$
  $- 3\frac{7}{8}$

$6\frac{6}{8}$

What's the Error?

> Dear Math Students,
>
> This is a problem from my math homework.
> My friend says my answer is not correct,
> but I can't figure out what I did wrong.
> Can you help me find and fix my mistake?
>
> Your friend,
> Puzzled Penguin

$4\frac{9}{8}$
$\cancel{4}\frac{1}{8}$
$- 1\frac{5}{8}$
$\overline{3\frac{4}{8}}$

29 Write a response to Puzzled Penguin.

_____

_____

_____

_____

Practice with Fractions and Mixed Numbers

Name _____

Real World Problems

Write an equation. Then solve.

Show your work.

30 Daniel spent $1\frac{1}{4}$ hours playing soccer on Saturday and $\frac{3}{4}$ hour playing soccer on Sunday. How much time did he spend playing soccer over the weekend?

_____

31 A pitcher contains $4\frac{3}{8}$ cups of juice. Antonio pours $\frac{5}{8}$ cup into a glass. How much juice is left in the pitcher?

_____

32 Shayna walked from school to the library. Then she walked $1\frac{3}{10}$ miles from the library to her apartment. If she walked $2\frac{1}{10}$ miles in all, how far did she walk from school to the library?

_____

33 The vet said Lucy's cat Mittens weighs $7\frac{1}{4}$ pounds. This is $1\frac{2}{4}$ pounds more than Mittens weighed last year. How much did Mittens weigh last year?

_____

34 The width of a rectangle is $3\frac{5}{6}$ inches. The length of the rectangle is $1\frac{4}{6}$ inches longer than the width. What is the length of the rectangle?

_____

35 Choose one of the problems on this page. Draw a model to show that your answer is correct.

Practice with Fractions and Mixed Numbers **271**

Make a Line Plot

36 Make a mark anywhere on this line segment.

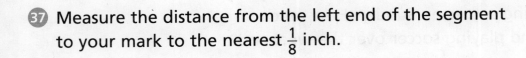

37 Measure the distance from the left end of the segment to your mark to the nearest $\frac{1}{8}$ inch.

_____

38 Collect measurements from your classmates and record them in the line plot below.

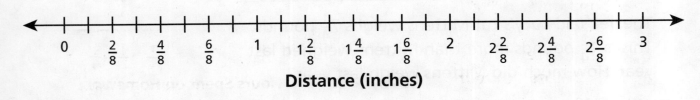

Distance (inches)

39 The range is the difference between the greatest value and the least value. What is the range of the data?

_____

40 Which distance value occurred most often?

_____

✓ Check Understanding

For your line plot in Problem 38, suppose the greatest value is $1\frac{4}{8}$ and the least value is $\frac{6}{8}$. What is the range of the data?

_____

Practice with Fractions and Mixed Numbers

Name

Date

Solve.

1   $3\frac{5}{6}$
    $+ 4\frac{5}{6}$

2   $9\frac{3}{10}$
    $- 2\frac{7}{10}$

Write an equation. Then solve.

Show your work.

3 A caterer serves 8 pies at a banquet. The people at the banquet eat $5\frac{4}{6}$ pies. How many pies are left?

_____

Solve.

4 The line plot shows the time Lina spent on homework during the past two weeks. What is the difference between the least amount of time and the greatest amount of time Lina spent on homework?

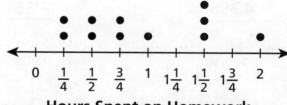

Hours Spent on Homework

_____

Write this fraction as a mixed number.

5 $\frac{23}{5}$

_____

Fluency Check 16

Name Date

PATH to FLUENCY

Add or subtract.

1. $142 + 557$

2. $6{,}703 - 5{,}281$

3. $6{,}836 + 742$

4. $76{,}294 - 5{,}926$

5. $37{,}982 + 31{,}856$

6. $486{,}793 + 78{,}319$

7. $3{,}278 + 4{,}396$

8. $742 - 361$

9. $829 + 155$

10. $60{,}508 - 26{,}774$

11. $884 - 371$

12. $87{,}314 + 32{,}975$

13. $745{,}298 - 51{,}889$

14. $5{,}976 - 3{,}513$

15. $807{,}963 - 348{,}279$

Name Naomi/Pebble

A Whole Number Multiplied by a Unit Fraction

The lunchroom at Mandy's school serves pizza every Friday. Each slice is $\frac{1}{4}$ of a pizza. Mandy eats one slice every week.

To find the fraction of a pizza she eats in three weeks, you can add or multiply.

$$\frac{1}{4} + \frac{1}{4} + \frac{1}{4} = \frac{3}{4} \quad \text{or} \quad 3 \cdot \frac{1}{4} = \frac{3}{4}$$

Solve each problem, first by adding and then by multiplying. Show your work.

1 What fraction of a pizza does she eat in five weeks?

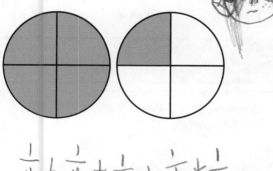

$$\frac{1}{4} + \frac{1}{4} + \frac{1}{4} + \frac{1}{4} + \frac{1}{4}$$

$$5 \cdot \frac{1}{4}$$

2 What fraction of a pizza does she eat in eleven weeks?

$$\frac{1}{4} + \frac{1}{4} + \frac{1}{4} + \frac{1}{4} + \frac{1}{4} + \frac{1}{4} + \frac{1}{4}$$

$$\frac{1}{4} + \frac{1}{4} + \frac{1}{4} + \frac{1}{4} \cdot 11 \cdot \frac{1}{4}$$

Draw a model for each problem. Then solve.

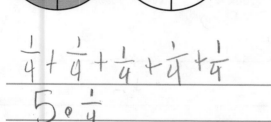

3 $2 \cdot \frac{1}{3} =$ $\frac{2}{4}$

4 $6 \cdot \frac{1}{5} =$ $\frac{6}{5}$

5 $10 \cdot \frac{1}{8} =$ $\frac{10}{6}$

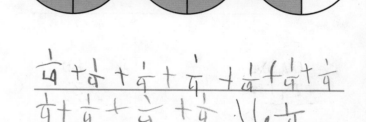

Draw a model for each fraction. Then write each fraction as the product of a whole number and a unit fraction.

6 $\frac{3}{5} =$ $3 \cdot \frac{1}{5}$

7 $\frac{8}{3} =$ $8 \cdot \frac{1}{3}$

8 $\frac{12}{7} =$ $12 \cdot \frac{1}{7}$

© Houghton Mifflin Harcourt Publishing Company

 Content Standards 4.NF.B.4, 4.NF.B.4.a, 4.NF.B.4.b, 4.NF.B.4.c, 4.MD.A.2
Mathematical Practices MP1, MP3, MP4, MP6

A Whole Number Multiplied by a Non-Unit Fraction

The lunchroom at Joe's school serves sub sandwiches every Thursday. Each slice is $\frac{1}{6}$ of a sub. Joe eats two pieces, or $\frac{2}{6}$ of a sandwich, every week.

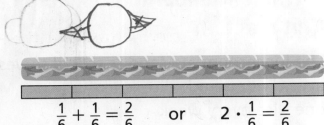

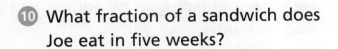

$$\frac{1}{6} + \frac{1}{6} = \frac{2}{6} \qquad \text{or} \qquad 2 \cdot \frac{1}{6} = \frac{2}{6}$$

Solve each problem, first by adding and then by multiplying. Write your answer as a fraction. Show your work.

9 What fraction of a sandwich does Joe eat in three weeks?

$$\frac{2}{6} + \frac{2}{6} + \frac{2}{6} = \frac{6}{6} = 1$$

$$3 \cdot \frac{2}{6} =$$

10 What fraction of a sandwich does Joe eat in five weeks?

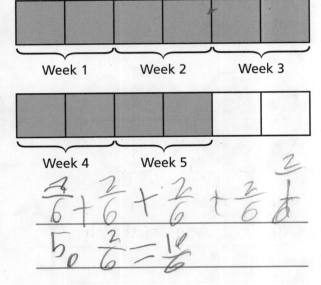

$$\frac{2}{6} + \frac{2}{6} + \frac{2}{6} + \frac{2}{6} \frac{2}{6}$$

$$5 \cdot \frac{2}{6} = \frac{10}{6}$$

Draw a model for each problem. Then solve.

11 $4 \cdot \frac{3}{8} = \dfrac{12}{8}$

12 $2 \cdot \frac{4}{5} = \dfrac{8}{5}$

13 $5 \cdot \frac{2}{3} = \dfrac{10}{3}$

Solve. Write your answer as a fraction.

14 $8 \cdot \frac{3}{4} = \dfrac{24}{4}$

15 $18 \cdot \frac{2}{3} = \dfrac{36}{3}$

16 $10 \cdot \frac{5}{6} = \dfrac{50}{6}$

17 $4 \cdot \frac{5}{7} = \dfrac{20}{7}$

18 $15 \cdot \frac{3}{10} = \dfrac{45}{10}$

19 $7 \cdot \frac{8}{9} = \dfrac{56}{9}$

Multiply a Fraction by a Whole Number

Real World Problems

Draw a model for each problem. Then solve.

20 The five members of the Sanchez family each drank
$\frac{3}{4}$ cup orange juice for breakfast. How much juice
did the family drink for breakfast altogether? _____

21 Stella ran $\frac{1}{2}$ mile. Brian ran 7 times as far as Stella.

How far did Brian run? _____

Write an equation. Then solve.   *Show your work.*

22 A banner has a length of 3 yards and a width of $\frac{2}{3}$ yard.
What is the area of the banner?

_____

23 The 12 members of a volleyball team had a pizza party.
Each pizza was divided into 8 equal slices and each player
ate 3 slices. How many pizzas did the team eat altogether?

_____

24 It took Eli's mother $\frac{1}{6}$ hour to drive him to school. It
took Alex 4 times as long as this to walk to school.
How long did it take Alex to walk to school?

_____

Real World Problems (continued)

Write an equation. Then solve.

Show your work.

25 Ami has building bricks that are $\frac{5}{8}$ inch thick. She makes a stack of 15 bricks. How tall is the stack?

_____

26 A crepe recipe calls for $\frac{3}{4}$ cup of flour. A bread recipe calls for four times this much flour. How much flour is in the bread recipe?

_____

What's the Error?

Dear Math Students,

I have so much homework! I have assignments in math, science, and reading. I think each subject will take $\frac{1}{2}$ hour. I tried to multiply to find the total time.

$3 \cdot \frac{1}{2} = \frac{3}{6}$

That can't be right! I know $\frac{3}{6}$ is the same as $\frac{1}{2}$ so that is only $\frac{1}{2}$ hour.

What did I do wrong? How long will my homework really take?

Your friend,
Puzzled Penguin

27 Write a response to Puzzled Penguin.

_____

_____

✓ **Check Understanding**

Draw a picture to show that $5 \cdot \frac{7}{12} = \frac{35}{12}$.

Multiply a Fraction by a Whole Number

Name _____

Multiplication Practice

Write each fraction as a sum of unit fractions and as the product of a whole number and a unit fraction.

1 $\frac{4}{7}$ = $\frac{1}{7} + \frac{1}{7} + \frac{1}{7} + \frac{1}{7}$

$\frac{4}{7}$ = $4 \cdot \frac{1}{7}$

2 $\frac{5}{2}$ = $\frac{1}{2} + \frac{1}{2} + \frac{1}{2} + \frac{1}{2} + \frac{1}{3}$

$\frac{5}{2}$ = $5 \cdot \frac{1}{2}$

3 $\frac{2}{3}$ =

$\frac{2}{3}$ =

4 $\frac{6}{4}$ =

$\frac{6}{4}$ =

Draw a model for each problem. Then solve.

5 $6 \cdot \frac{1}{4}$ = $\frac{6}{4}$

6 $6 \cdot \frac{2}{3}$ = $\frac{12}{3}$

7 $3 \cdot \frac{2}{9}$ = $\frac{6}{9}$

8 $4 \cdot \frac{4}{5}$ = $\frac{16}{5}$

Multiply. Write your answer as a mixed number or a whole number, when possible.

9 $20 \cdot \frac{3}{10}$ = $\frac{60}{10}$ $\frac{4}{12}$

10 $36 \cdot \frac{5}{9}$ = $\frac{180}{9} = 20$ $^{36}_{\times 5}$

11 $2 \cdot \frac{2}{12}$ =

12 $21 \cdot \frac{1}{3}$ =

13 $16 \cdot \frac{3}{8}$ = 48

14 $11 \cdot \frac{7}{10}$ =

CC SS Content Standards 4.NF.B.4, 4.NF.B.4.a, 4.NF.B.4.b, 4.NF.B.4.c, 4.MD.A.2
Mathematical Practices MP3, MP4, MP6

Practice Multiplying a Fraction by a Whole Number **279**

Real World Problems

Show your work.

Draw a model for each problem. Then solve. Write your answer as a mixed number or a whole number, when possible.

15 Michelle has three textbooks. Each weighs $\frac{5}{8}$ pound. What is the total weight of her textbooks?

_____

16 Mark lived in a house in the suburbs with $\frac{2}{3}$ acre of land. Then he moved to a farm in the country that has 6 times as much land. How much land is on Mark's farm?

_____

Write an equation. Then solve. Write your answer as a mixed number or a whole number, when possible.

17 A restaurant served quiche for lunch today. Each quiche was cut into six equal pieces. The restaurant sold 59 pieces. How many quiches is this?

_____

18 Zahra's dog Brutus weighed $\frac{7}{8}$ pound when he was born. Now he weighs 60 times as much. How much does Brutus weigh now?

_____

19 Calvin made posters to advertise the school play. Each poster is 2 feet long and $\frac{11}{12}$ foot wide. What is the area of each poster?

_____

✓ **Check Understanding**

Explain why the denominator does not change when you multiply a fraction by a whole number.

Practice Multiplying a Fraction by a Whole Number

Name _____

Practice Fraction Operations

Write each fraction as a sum of fractions in two different ways.

1. $\frac{3}{10}$ = $\frac{1}{10} + \frac{2}{10}$ $\frac{2}{10} + \frac{1}{10}$

2. $\frac{7}{7}$ = $\frac{5}{7} + \frac{2}{7}$, $\frac{6}{7} + \frac{1}{7}$

3. $\frac{4}{5}$ = $\frac{2}{5} + \frac{2}{9}$, $\frac{3}{5} + \frac{1}{5}$

4. $\frac{5}{12}$ = $\frac{4}{12} + \frac{1}{12}$, $\frac{3}{12} + \frac{2}{12}$

Add or subtract.

5. $\frac{5}{8} + \frac{3}{8}$ = $\frac{8}{8} = 1$

6. $\frac{2}{10} + \frac{1}{10}$ = $\frac{3}{10}$

7. $\frac{7}{9} - \frac{3}{9}$ = $\frac{4}{9}$

8. $6\frac{7}{10}$
   $- 1\frac{4}{10}$
   $\frac{3}{10}$

9. $5\frac{2}{3}$
   $+ 4\frac{1}{3}$
   $10\frac{3}{3} = 1$

10. $6\frac{1}{6}$
    $- 3\frac{2}{6}$
    $3\frac{5}{6}$ $\frac{6}{6} = \frac{7}{6}$

11. $12\frac{4}{9}$
    $+ 10\frac{5}{9}$
    $23 \frac{9}{9} = 1$

12. $1\frac{4}{5}$
    $+ 1\frac{3}{5}$
    $\frac{7}{5}$ $\frac{5}{5} - \frac{3}{5}$ $1\frac{1}{4}$ $5\frac{3}{4}$

Multiply. Write your answer as a mixed number or a whole number, when possible.

14. $7 \cdot \frac{1}{10}$ = $\frac{7}{10}$

15. $4 \cdot \frac{2}{9}$ = $\frac{8}{9}$

16. $5 \cdot \frac{3}{5}$ = $\frac{15}{5}$

17. $12 \cdot \frac{3}{4}$ = $\frac{36}{4} = 9$

18. $7 \cdot \frac{5}{8}$ = $\frac{35}{8} = 14\frac{3}{8}$

19. $10 \cdot \frac{5}{6}$ = $\frac{50}{6} = 8\frac{2}{6}$

Content Standards 4.NF.B.3.b, 4.NF.B.3.c, 4.NF.B.3.d, 4.NF.B.4.b, 4.NF.B.4.c, 4.MD.A.2 Mathematical Practices MP3, MP6, MP8

Mixed Practice **281**

Real World Problems

Write an equation. Then solve.   *Show your work.*

20 Dimitri rode his bike 32 miles yesterday. He rode $12\frac{4}{5}$ miles before lunch and the rest of the distance after lunch. How far did he ride after lunch?

_____

21 Ms. Washington is taking an accounting class. Each class is $\frac{3}{4}$ hour long. If there are 22 classes in all, how many hours will Ms. Washington spend in class?

_____

22 Elin bought a large watermelon at the farmers market. She cut off a $5\frac{5}{8}$-pound piece and gave it to her neighbor. She has $11\frac{5}{8}$ pounds of watermelon left. How much did the whole watermelon weigh?

_____

23 A bread recipe calls for $\frac{3}{4}$ cup of whole wheat flour, $1\frac{2}{4}$ cups of white flour, and $\frac{3}{4}$ cup of rye flour. How much flour is this in all?

_____

24 Henri spent a total of $3\frac{2}{6}$ hours working on his science project. Kali spent $1\frac{5}{6}$ hours working on her science project. How much longer did Henri work on his project?

_____

25 A track is $\frac{1}{4}$ mile long. Kenny ran around the track 21 times. How far did Kenny run in all?

_____

✓**Check Understanding**

Which problem above could you ungroup a whole number to find the difference?

_____

Mixed Practice

Name _____

Math and Vegetarian Pizza Farms

A pizza farm is a circular region of land divided into eight pie-shaped wedges or slices, such as those you would see in a pizza. At a vegetarian pizza farm, each wedge or slice grows a different vegetarian ingredient used to make a pizza. Some things you might find on a vegetarian pizza farm include wheat, fruit, vegetables, Italian herbs, and dairy cows to make cheese.

Write an equation to solve.

Show your work.

A farmer created a vegetarian pizza farm with these wedges or slices: $\frac{3}{8}$ for vegetables, $\frac{1}{8}$ for wheat, $\frac{2}{8}$ for fruit, $\frac{1}{8}$ for dairy cows, and $\frac{1}{8}$ for Italian herbs.

1 What fraction of the farm is made up of fruit or vegetables?

_____

2 What fraction of the farm is *not* made up of wheat?

_____

3 Which wedge of the farm is bigger, the wedge for fruit or the wedge for Italian herbs? Explain.

_____

Write an equation to solve.

Show your work.

4 On Monday, two of the workers at the pizza farm each filled a basket with ripe tomatoes. Miles picked $15\frac{1}{6}$ pounds of tomatoes, and Anna picked $13\frac{5}{6}$ pounds of tomatoes. How many more pounds of tomatoes did Miles pick than Anna?

_____

For Problems 5–6, use the line plot to solve.

After a field trip to a vegetarian pizza farm, Mrs. Cannon asked each of her students to use some of their study time to research different vegetarian ingredients for pizzas. The line plot below shows the amount of time each student spent researching during study time.

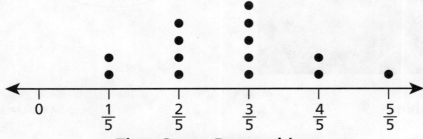

Time Spent Researching During Study Time (in hours)

5 How many students spent at least $\frac{3}{5}$ hour researching? Explain how you know.

_____

_____

6 How many hours in all did the students who researched for $\frac{2}{5}$ hour spend researching? Write a multiplication equation to solve.

_____

Focus on Mathematical Practices

Multiply.

1 $10 \cdot \frac{2}{10} =$ _____

2 $13 \cdot \frac{5}{8} =$ _____

3 Liam has two trophies. The first trophy weighs $\frac{3}{8}$ pound. The second trophy weighs 3 times as much as the first trophy. How much does the second trophy weigh?

Show your work.

_____

Write an equation. Then solve.

4 Cassie works on her art project $\frac{3}{4}$ hour every day for 12 days. How many hours does Cassie work on her project altogether?

_____

5 At a petting zoo, $\frac{2}{12}$ of the animals are sheep and $\frac{5}{12}$ are goats. What fraction of the animals at the petting zoo are sheep or goats?

_____

Name _____ **Date** _____

Add or subtract.

1
$$\begin{array}{r} 6{,}894 \\ -\ 3{,}421 \\ \hline \end{array}$$

2
$$\begin{array}{r} 472 \\ -\ 368 \\ \hline \end{array}$$

3
$$\begin{array}{r} 7{,}086 \\ -\ 4{,}825 \\ \hline \end{array}$$

4
$$\begin{array}{r} 1{,}176 \\ +\ \ 483 \\ \hline \end{array}$$

5
$$\begin{array}{r} 345 \\ +\ 314 \\ \hline \end{array}$$

6
$$\begin{array}{r} 354{,}964 \\ -\ \ 46{,}379 \\ \hline \end{array}$$

7
$$\begin{array}{r} 76{,}429 \\ +\ \ 6{,}850 \\ \hline \end{array}$$

8
$$\begin{array}{r} 62{,}000 \\ -\ 51{,}752 \\ \hline \end{array}$$

9
$$\begin{array}{r} 205{,}782 \\ -\ 178{,}935 \\ \hline \end{array}$$

10
$$\begin{array}{r} 798 \\ -\ 340 \\ \hline \end{array}$$

11
$$\begin{array}{r} 45{,}284 \\ -\ \ 8{,}451 \\ \hline \end{array}$$

12
$$\begin{array}{r} 84{,}275 \\ +\ 17{,}682 \\ \hline \end{array}$$

13
$$\begin{array}{r} 725 \\ +\ 644 \\ \hline \end{array}$$

14
$$\begin{array}{r} 295{,}930 \\ +\ 357{,}392 \\ \hline \end{array}$$

15
$$\begin{array}{r} 8{,}312 \\ +\ 7{,}548 \\ \hline \end{array}$$

1. Represent the shaded part of the fraction bar as the product of a whole number and a unit fraction.

| $\frac{1}{8}$ | $\frac{1}{8}$ | $\frac{1}{8}$ | $\frac{1}{8}$ | $\frac{1}{8}$ | $\frac{1}{8}$ | $\frac{1}{8}$ | $\frac{1}{8}$ |

$$6 \cdot \frac{1}{8}$$

2. In the morning Naomi jumps rope for $\frac{1}{4}$ hour. After lunch she jumps rope for another $\frac{2}{4}$ hour. How long does Naomi jump rope? Write an equation. Then solve.

Equation: $\frac{1}{4} + \frac{2}{4}$

Solution: $\frac{2}{4}$ hour

3. For Exercises 3a–3d, write a fraction from the tiles to make a true equation.

$\frac{1}{10}$ $\frac{2}{10}$ $\frac{3}{10}$ $\frac{4}{10}$

3a. $\frac{10}{10} = \frac{5}{10} + \frac{3}{10} +$ $\frac{2}{10}$

3c. $\frac{7}{10} = \frac{1}{10} + \frac{1}{10} + \frac{1}{10} + \frac{1}{10} +$ $\frac{3}{10}$

3b. $1 = \frac{1}{10} + \frac{5}{10} +$ $\frac{4}{10}$

3d. $\frac{4}{10} = \frac{1}{10} + \frac{1}{10} + \frac{1}{10} +$ $\frac{1}{10}$

4 Caesar buys dog treats and cat treats. He buys $\frac{7}{8}$ pound of dog treats. This is $\frac{5}{8}$ pound more than the weight of the cat treats he buys. How many pounds of cat treats does Caesar buy? Write an equation. Then solve.

Equation: $\frac{7-5}{8\ 8}$

Solution: $\frac{2}{8}$ _____ pound

5 A recipe calls for $\frac{2}{3}$ cup of mushrooms. Dae uses 3 times as many cups of mushrooms. Choose the number of cups of mushrooms he uses. Mark all that apply.

Ⓐ $\frac{5}{3}$ cups   Ⓒ 2 cups

Ⓑ $\frac{6}{3}$ cups   Ⓓ 3 cups

$\frac{3 \cdot 2}{3} = \frac{6}{3}$

$3\overline{)6}$

6 Complete the table to show the fraction as a product of a whole number and a unit fraction.

Fraction	Product
$\frac{5}{12}$	$5 \cdot \frac{1}{12}$
$\frac{2}{3}$	$2 \cdot \frac{1}{3}$
$\frac{4}{5}$	$4 \cdot \frac{1}{5}$

7 For 7a–7d, choose the operation that makes the equation true.

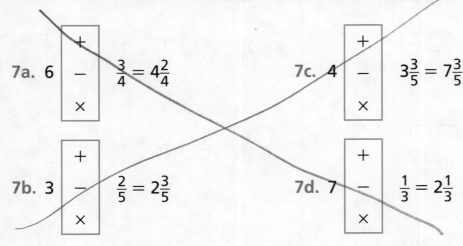

7a. 6 [+ − ×] $\frac{3}{4} = 4\frac{2}{4}$

7b. 3 [+ − ×] $\frac{2}{5} = 2\frac{3}{5}$

7c. 4 [+ − ×] $3\frac{3}{5} = 7\frac{3}{5}$

7d. 7 [+ − ×] $\frac{1}{3} = 2\frac{1}{3}$

8 Multiply the expression to complete the table.

Expression	Written as a Fraction	Written as a Mixed Number
$7 \cdot \frac{1}{6}$	$\frac{7}{6}$	$1\frac{1}{6}$
$12 \cdot \frac{1}{5}$	$\frac{12}{5}$	$2\frac{2}{5}$
$3 \cdot \frac{5}{8}$	$\frac{15}{8}$	$1\frac{7}{8}$

9 For Exercises 9a–9f, choose True or False for the equation.

9a. $\frac{2}{8} + \frac{1}{8} = \frac{3}{16}$ ○ True   ○ False

9b. $\frac{4}{5} - \frac{1}{5} = \frac{3}{5}$ ○ True   ○ False

9c. $\frac{9}{4} + \frac{2}{4} = 2\frac{3}{4}$ ○ True   ○ False

9d. $\frac{5}{12} + \frac{4}{12} = \frac{9}{24}$ ○ True   ○ False

9e. $8\frac{5}{6} - 6\frac{4}{6} = 2\frac{1}{6}$ ○ True   ○ False

9f. $2\frac{7}{10} + 3\frac{3}{10} = 5\frac{10}{20}$ ○ True   ○ False

10 Elias says this problem can be solved using addition. Vladimir says it can be solved using multiplication. Explain why both boys are correct.

Milo practices piano $\frac{3}{5}$ hour every day. How many hours does he practice in 5 days?

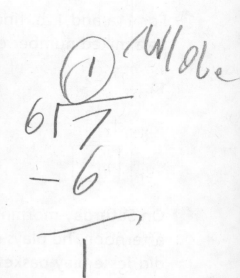

11 For 11a and 11b, find the sum or difference. Write your answer as a mixed number or a whole number, when possible.

11a.
$$5\frac{2}{3}$$
$$+\ 4\frac{2}{3}$$
$$\boxed{}$$

11b.
$$9\frac{3}{8}$$
$$-\ 3\frac{7}{8}$$
$$\boxed{}$$

12 On Saturday morning, Jesse plays basketball for $\frac{2}{3}$ hour. In the afternoon, he plays some more. He plays $2\frac{1}{3}$ hours in all. How long did Jesse play basketball in the afternoon?

Part A

Draw a model to represent the problem. Then solve. Explain how your model helps you solve the problem.

Part B

On Sunday, Jesse played basketball for $1\frac{2}{3}$ hours. How many total hours did he play basketball on Saturday and Sunday? Show your work.

13 Rebecca's soup recipe calls for $\frac{3}{4}$ cup of milk. She needs 3 times as much milk to make a triple batch of soup. How many cups of milk does Rebecca need?

Part A

Draw a model for the problem.

Part B

Use your model to write two equations for the problem. Then solve.

14 For Exercises 14a–14e, choose Yes or No to tell whether the addition equation is true.

14a. $\frac{8}{10} = \frac{5}{10} + \frac{3}{10}$ ○ Yes ○ No

14b. $\frac{4}{5} = \frac{1}{5} + \frac{1}{5} + \frac{1}{5} + \frac{1}{5} + \frac{1}{5}$ ○ Yes ○ No

14c. $\frac{6}{11} = \frac{4}{6} + \frac{2}{5}$ ○ Yes ○ No

14d. $\frac{3}{8} = \frac{1}{8} + \frac{1}{8} + \frac{1}{8}$ ○ Yes ○ No

14e. $\frac{10}{12} = \frac{5}{12} + \frac{5}{12}$ ○ Yes ○ No

15 The line plot shows the lengths of trails Andrea hiked last month at a state park.

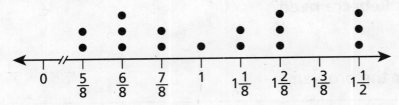

Trail Lengths (miles)

Andrea hiked 3 miles last week. She could have hiked two $1\frac{1}{2}$-mile trails. Describe two other combinations of trails she could have hiked.

16 Select the expression that is equivalent to $2\frac{2}{6}$. Mark all that apply.

Ⓐ $\frac{1}{6} + \frac{1}{6} + \frac{2}{6}$

Ⓓ $\frac{6}{6} + \frac{6}{6} + \frac{1}{6} + \frac{1}{6}$

Ⓑ $1 + 1 + \frac{2}{6}$

Ⓔ $\frac{20}{6} + \frac{2}{6}$

Ⓒ $\frac{2}{6} + \frac{2}{6} + \frac{2}{6}$

Ⓕ $\frac{6}{6} + \frac{3}{6} + \frac{3}{6} + \frac{2}{6}$

17 Explain how to change $\frac{11}{4}$ to a mixed number.

Mixing Paint

Mr. Myers stores paint in equal-size jars in his classroom.
The table shows the amount of each color he has.

Mr. Myers's Paint						
Color	Red	Orange	Yellow	Blue	Green	Purple
Amount of Jar Filled	1	$\frac{1}{8}$	$1\frac{2}{8}$	$\frac{4}{8}$	$\frac{3}{8}$	$\frac{7}{8}$

1 Janet's project requires $\frac{5}{8}$ of a jar of orange paint.
To make more orange, she needs to combine equal parts
of red and yellow. How much of each color does she need?

_____

_____

_____

2 How much red paint is left? How much yellow paint is left?

_____

_____

3 Three students need purple paint. Show how Mr. Myers
can divide all of the paint into three jars. If he wants the
three jars to contain an equal amount of paint, how much
will be in each jar? How much will be left over?

_____

_____

_____

_____

4 Emilio's project used all the green paint in the jar, but his project is not finished. Mr. Myers thinks that Emilio needs 3 times as much green paint as he started with to finish. To make green, equal parts of yellow and blue can be combined. Does Mr. Myers have enough paint to make the amount of green paint Emilio needs? Explain why or why not.

_____

_____

_____

5 Mr. Myers decides to buy green paint instead of making it. How many full jars of green paint does he need to buy? Explain.

_____

_____

6 At the end of the class, Mr. Meyers has $\frac{4}{8}$ jar of red paint and $\frac{5}{8}$ jar of yellow paint, and no orange paint. He finds $\frac{6}{8}$ of another jar of red paint in the closet. He wants to combine both jars of red paint to make one full jar and use any remaining red paint to mix with an equal amount of yellow paint to make more orange paint. How much red, yellow, and orange paint will he have? Explain how you solved the problem.

_____

_____

_____

Dear Family:

In Lessons 1 through 7 of Unit 7 of *Math Expressions*, your child will build on previous experience with fractions. Your child will use both physical models and numerical methods to recognize and to find fractions equivalent to a given fraction. Your child will also compare fractions and mixed numbers, including those with like and unlike numerators and denominators.

By using fraction strips, students determine how to model and compare fractions, and to find equivalent fractions. Your child will also learn how to use multiplication and division to find equivalent fractions.

Examples of Fraction Bar Modeling:

Fraction Comparisons

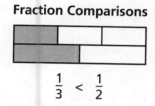

$$\frac{1}{3} < \frac{1}{2}$$

Equivalent Fractions

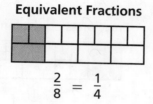

$$\frac{2}{8} = \frac{1}{4}$$

Your child will be introduced to the number-line model for fractions. Students name fractions corresponding to given lengths on the number line and identify lengths corresponding to given fractions. They also see that there are many equivalent fraction names for any given length.

Your child will apply this knowledge of fractions to word problems and in data displays.

If you have questions or problems, please contact me.

Thank you.

Sincerely,
Your child's teacher

CC SS Unit 7 addresses the following standards from the Common Core State Standards for Mathematics: **4.NF.A.1, 4.NF.A.2, 4.NF.C.5, 4.NF.C.6, 4.NF.C.7, 4.MD.A.2, 4.MD.B.4, and all** Mathematical Practices.

Estimada familia:

En las lecciones 1 a 7 de la Unidad 7 de *Math Expressions*, el niño ampliará sus conocimientos previos acerca de las fracciones. Su niño usará modelos físicos y métodos numéricos para reconocer y hallar fracciones equivalentes para una fracción dada. También comparará fracciones y números mixtos, incluyendo aquellos que tengan numeradores y denominadores iguales o diferentes.

Usando tiras de fracciones, los estudiantes determinarán cómo hacer modelos y comparar fracciones y cómo hallar fracciones equivalentes. Además, aprenderán cómo usar la multiplicación y división para hallar fracciones equivalentes.

Ejemplos de modelos con barras de fracciones:

Comparar fracciones

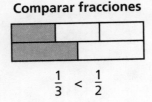

$$\frac{1}{3} < \frac{1}{2}$$

Fracciones equivalentes

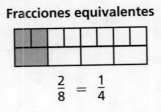

$$\frac{2}{8} = \frac{1}{4}$$

Su niño estudiará por primera vez el modelo de recta numérica para las fracciones. Los estudiantes nombrarán las fracciones que correspondan a determinadas longitudes en la recta numérica e identificarán longitudes que correspondan a fracciones dadas. También observarán que hay muchos nombres de fracciones equivalentes para una longitud determinada.

Su niño aplicará este conocimiento de las fracciones en problemas y en presentaciones de datos.

Si tiene alguna duda o algún comentario, por favor comuníquese conmigo.

Atentamente,
El maestro de su niño

CC SS En la Unidad 7 se aplican los siguientes estándares de los Estándares estatales comunes de matemáticas: **4.NF.A.1, 4.NF.A.2, 4.NF.C.5, 4.NF.C.6, 4.NF.C.7, 4.MD.A.2, 4.MD.B.4 y todos los de** Prácticas matemáticas.

Compare Fractions

common denominator

hundredth

decimal number

simplify a fraction

equivalent fractions

tenth

A unit fraction representing one of one hundred parts, written as 0.01 or $\frac{1}{100}$.

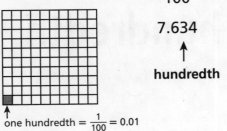

7.634

↑

hundredth

one hundredth = $\frac{1}{100}$ = 0.01

A common multiple of two or more denominators.

Example:
A common denominator of $\frac{1}{2}$ and $\frac{1}{3}$ is 6 because 6 is a multiple of 2 and 3.

Dividing the numerator and the denominator of a fraction by the same number to make an equivalent fraction made from fewer but larger unit fractions.

Example:
$\frac{5}{10} = \frac{5 \div 5}{10 \div 5} = \frac{1}{2}$

A representation of a number using the numerals 0 to 9, in which each digit has a value 10 times the digit to its right. A dot or **decimal point** separates the whole-number part of the number on the left from the fractional part on the right.

Example:
1.23 and 0.3

A unit fraction representing one of ten equal parts of a whole, written as 0.1 or $\frac{1}{10}$.

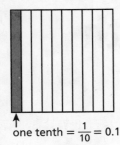

12.34

↑

tenth

one tenth = $\frac{1}{10}$ = 0.1

Two or more fractions that represent the same number.

Example:
$\frac{2}{4}$ and $\frac{4}{8}$ are equivalent because they both represent one half.

$\frac{1}{1}$ $\frac{1}{1}$

$\frac{1}{2}$ $\frac{1}{2}$ $\frac{2}{2}$

$\frac{1}{3}$ $\frac{1}{3}$ $\frac{1}{3}$ $\frac{3}{3}$

$\frac{1}{4}$ $\frac{1}{4}$ $\frac{1}{4}$ $\frac{1}{4}$ $\frac{4}{4}$

$\frac{1}{5}$ $\frac{1}{5}$ $\frac{1}{5}$ $\frac{1}{5}$ $\frac{1}{5}$ $\frac{5}{5}$

$\frac{1}{6}$ $\frac{1}{6}$ $\frac{1}{6}$ $\frac{1}{6}$ $\frac{1}{6}$ $\frac{1}{6}$ $\frac{6}{6}$

$\frac{1}{7}$ $\frac{1}{7}$ $\frac{1}{7}$ $\frac{1}{7}$ $\frac{1}{7}$ $\frac{1}{7}$ $\frac{1}{7}$ $\frac{7}{7}$

$\frac{1}{8}$ $\frac{1}{8}$ $\frac{1}{8}$ $\frac{1}{8}$ $\frac{1}{8}$ $\frac{1}{8}$ $\frac{1}{8}$ $\frac{1}{8}$ $\frac{8}{8}$

$\frac{1}{9}$ $\frac{1}{9}$ $\frac{1}{9}$ $\frac{1}{9}$ $\frac{1}{9}$ $\frac{1}{9}$ $\frac{1}{9}$ $\frac{1}{9}$ $\frac{1}{9}$ $\frac{9}{9}$

$\frac{1}{10}$ (×10) $\frac{10}{10}$

$\frac{1}{11}$ (×11) $\frac{11}{11}$

$\frac{1}{12}$ (×12) $\frac{12}{12}$

$\frac{1}{13}$ (×13) $\frac{13}{13}$

$\frac{1}{14}$ (×14) $\frac{14}{14}$

$\frac{1}{15}$ (×15) $\frac{15}{15}$

$\frac{1}{16}$ (×16) $\frac{16}{16}$

$\frac{1}{17}$ (×17) $\frac{17}{17}$

$\frac{1}{18}$ (×18) $\frac{18}{18}$

$\frac{1}{19}$ (×19) $\frac{19}{19}$

$\frac{1}{20}$ (×20) $\frac{20}{20}$

Compare Fractions

Name _____

Practice Comparing Fractions

Circle the greater fraction. Use fraction strips if you need to.

1. $\frac{1}{12}$ or $\frac{1}{2}$

2. $\frac{3}{8}$ or $\frac{1}{8}$

3. $\frac{2}{5}$ or $\frac{2}{6}$

4. $\frac{1}{3}$ or $\frac{1}{5}$

5. $\frac{4}{12}$ or $\frac{5}{12}$

6. $\frac{7}{10}$ or $\frac{5}{10}$

7. $\frac{1}{3}$ or $\frac{2}{3}$

8. $\frac{3}{6}$ or $\frac{3}{8}$

Write > or < to make each statement true.

9. $\frac{3}{10}$ ◯ $\frac{3}{8}$

10. $\frac{3}{6}$ ◯ $\frac{3}{5}$

11. $\frac{8}{10}$ ◯ $\frac{8}{12}$

12. $\frac{2}{6}$ ◯ $\frac{3}{6}$

13. $\frac{7}{10}$ ◯ $\frac{7}{8}$

14. $\frac{5}{100}$ ◯ $\frac{4}{100}$

What's the Error?

Dear Math Students,

Yesterday, my family caught a large fish. We ate $\frac{2}{6}$ of the fish. Today, we ate $\frac{2}{4}$ of the fish. I told my mother that we ate more fish yesterday than today because 6 is greater than 4, so $\frac{2}{6}$ is greater than $\frac{2}{4}$. My mother told me I made a mistake. Can you help me to figure out what my mistake was?

Your friend,
Puzzled Penguin

15. Write a response to Puzzled Penguin.

_____

_____

_____

_____

Make Sense of Problems

16 Explain how to compare fractions with the same denominator but different numerators.

_____

_____

17 Explain how to compare fractions with the same numerator but different denominators.

_____

_____

Solve.

18 Bao listed the birds that visited his bird feeder Friday. He said that $\frac{2}{5}$ were finches and $\frac{2}{6}$ were wrens. Did more finches or more wrens visit the bird feeder? Explain.

_____

_____

19 Mariel had a box of baseball cards. She kept $\frac{3}{8}$ of the cards and gave $\frac{5}{8}$ of the cards to Javier. Who had more of the cards? Explain.

_____

_____

20 Write the fractions $\frac{10}{12}$, $\frac{5}{12}$, and $\frac{7}{12}$ in order from least to greatest.

_____

✔**Check Understanding**
Draw a diagram to support your solution to Problem 19.

Compare Fractions

Name

Discuss Number Lines

The number line below shows the fourths between 0 and 1. Discuss how the number line is like and unlike the fraction bar above it.

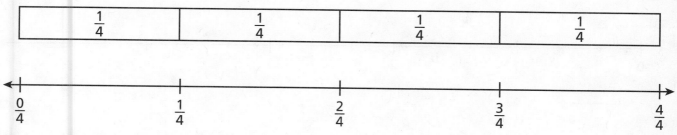

These number lines are divided to show different fractions.

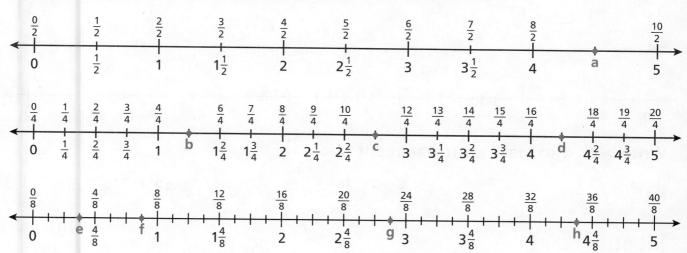

Write > or < to make each statement true.

1 $\frac{3}{4}$ ◯ $\frac{5}{2}$ **2** $\frac{15}{4}$ ◯ $\frac{20}{8}$ **3** $\frac{10}{4}$ ◯ $\frac{24}{8}$ **4** $2\frac{4}{8}$ ◯ $1\frac{3}{4}$

Identify Points

5 Write the fraction or mixed number for each lettered point on the number lines above.

a. _____   b. _____   c. _____   d. _____

e. _____   f. _____   g. _____   h. _____

Number Lines for Thirds and Sixths

Tell how many equal parts are between 0 and 1.
Then write fraction labels above the equal parts.

6 _____

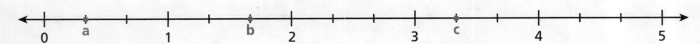

7 _____

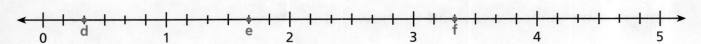

8 _____

Write > or < to make each statement true.

9 $\frac{4}{3}$ ◯ $\frac{7}{6}$ **10** $\frac{8}{3}$ ◯ $\frac{18}{6}$ **11** $3\frac{5}{6}$ ◯ $3\frac{2}{3}$

Identify Points

12 Write the fraction or mixed number for each lettered
point above. Describe any patterns you see with the class.

a. _____   b. _____   c. _____

d. _____   e. _____   f. _____

g. _____   h. _____   i. _____

Mark and label the letter of each fraction or
mixed number on the number line.

13

a. $\frac{1}{5}$ b. $\frac{7}{10}$ c. $1\frac{2}{5}$ d. $2\frac{1}{2}$

e. $3\frac{3}{10}$ f. $4\frac{2}{5}$ g. $4\frac{9}{10}$ h. $5\frac{1}{2}$

Fractions on the Number Line

Name _____

Fractions and Benchmarks

Decide if each fraction is closer to 0 or closer to 1.
Write *closer to 0* or *closer to 1*.

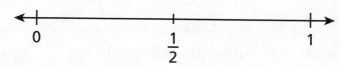

$$0 \qquad \frac{1}{2} \qquad 1$$

14 $\frac{1}{4}$ _____

15 $\frac{3}{4}$ _____

16 $\frac{7}{8}$ _____

Write > or < to make each statement true.

17 $\frac{5}{8}$ ◯ $\frac{11}{12}$

18 $\frac{7}{12}$ ◯ $\frac{1}{8}$

19 $\frac{3}{8}$ ◯ $\frac{1}{6}$

What's the Error?

Dear Math Students,

I am baking cookies. My recipe calls for $\frac{5}{8}$ pound of walnuts. Walnuts come in $\frac{1}{2}$-pound bags and 1-pound bags. My friend says that $\frac{5}{8}$ is closer to $\frac{1}{2}$ than it is to 1, so I should buy a $\frac{1}{2}$-pound bag. I think my friend is wrong.

Do you agree with me or with my friend? Can you help me decide what size bag of walnuts I should buy?

Your friend,
Puzzled Penguin

20 Write a response to Puzzled Penguin.

_____

_____

_____

_____

Use Benchmarks

The list below shows a variety of cooking ingredients and amounts.

Ingredients and Amounts (c = cup)	
wheat flour $1\frac{5}{8}$ c	white flour $\frac{4}{6}$ c
sugar $1\frac{1}{8}$ c	cornstarch $\frac{3}{8}$ c
oat bran $1\frac{4}{5}$ c	water $\frac{2}{6}$ c

Decide if each amount is closer to $\frac{1}{2}$ cup, $1\frac{1}{2}$ cups, or 2 cups.
Write *closer to $\frac{1}{2}$ c*, *closer to $1\frac{1}{2}$ c*, or *closer to 2 c*.

21 wheat flour _____

22 white flour _____

23 sugar _____

24 cornstarch _____

25 oat bran _____

26 water _____

Decide which ingredient represents a greater amount.

27 sugar or water _____

28 sugar or wheat flour _____

29 cornstarch or sugar _____

30 wheat flour or white flour _____

31 sugar or oat bran _____

32 oat bran or white flour _____

✔ **Check Understanding**

Which is greater, $\frac{3}{8}$ or $\frac{5}{4}$? Draw a number line to show your solution.

Name _____

Compare Fractions of Different-Size Wholes

Jon and his five friends want sandwiches. They make two sandwiches: one on a short loaf of bread and one on a longer loaf. Jon cuts each sandwich into 6 equal pieces. His friends think the pieces are not the same size.

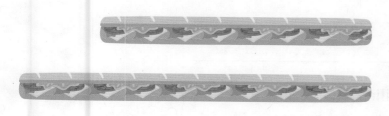

1 Are Jon's friends correct? Explain.

_____

_____

_____

2 What can Jon do to make sure everyone gets the same amount of food?

_____

_____

Hattie's dad orders one small, one medium, and one large pizza. He divides each pizza into 8 equal pieces. Hattie takes $\frac{1}{8}$ of the small pizza and her friend takes $\frac{1}{8}$ of the large pizza.

 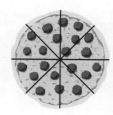 

3 Hattie says she has less pizza than her friend. Is she correct? Explain.

_____

_____

_____

4 What do these problems tell us about fractions?

_____

© Houghton Mifflin Harcourt Publishing Company

Fraction Word Problems

Show your work.

5 A shelter had 4 spaniel puppies and 6 beagle puppies. Jack adopted $\frac{1}{2}$ of the spaniel puppies, and Carmen adopted $\frac{1}{2}$ of the beagle puppies. Who adopted more puppies? How do you know?

_____

_____

6 Julio planted 16 daisies and 10 lilies. His goat ate 5 daisies and 5 lilies. Did the goat eat a greater fractional part of the daisies or the lilies? Explain.

_____

_____

7 A fruit market sells two different packages of oranges. Bags contain 12 oranges, and boxes contain 15 oranges. Both packages cost $5.00. Which package is a better buy? Why?

_____

_____

8 The fourth grade has three running teams. Each team has 12 runners. In a race, $\frac{1}{4}$ of Team A, $\frac{1}{3}$ of Team B, and $\frac{1}{6}$ of Team C passed the first water stop at the same time. Which team had the most runners at the first water stop at that time? Explain.

_____

_____

✓**Check Understanding**

Circle the word to complete the sentence. When the wholes are different and the fractions are the same, the fractional part of the *smaller/larger* whole is greater.

© Houghton Mifflin Harcourt Publishing Company

Fractions of Different-Size Wholes

Write >, <, or = to make the statement true.

1. $\frac{3}{5}$ ◯ $\frac{3}{8}$

2. $\frac{3}{8}$ ◯ $\frac{5}{8}$

3. Label the point for each fraction or mixed number with the corresponding letter.

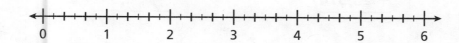

0   1   2   3   4   5   6

a. $3\frac{1}{2}$ b. $2\frac{1}{3}$ c. $\frac{2}{3}$ d. $5\frac{5}{6}$ e. $1\frac{1}{6}$

Which fraction or mixed number is closest to 1?

_____

Solve.   *Show your work.*

4. Cory ships two paperback books. One weighs $\frac{3}{8}$ pound and the other weighs $\frac{3}{4}$ pound. Which weight is greater than $\frac{1}{2}$ pound?

_____

5. A farmer has 8 horses and 12 cows. He put $\frac{1}{4}$ of the horses in the barn and $\frac{1}{4}$ of the cows in the barn. Did he put more horses or cows in the barn? Explain.

_____

_____

Name _____ **Date** _____

Add or subtract.

1. 2,156
   + 4,869

2. 478
   − 386

3. 3,742
   + 823

4. 7,968
   − 3,526

5. 54,683
   + 23,574

6. 475,498
   − 88,532

7. 605,748
   − 349,582

8. 537
   − 315

9. 836
   + 753

10. 86,334
    − 3,782

11. 145
    + 232

12. 47,542
    + 8,750

13. 80,000
    − 34,689

14. 586,456
    + 56,967

15. 7,603
    − 4,421

Name Naomi/Pebble

Equivalent Fractions

VOCABULARY
equivalent fractions

Read and discuss the problem situation.

Lewis works summers at Maria's Fruit Farm. One day, Maria agreed to give Lewis extra pay if he could sell $\frac{2}{3}$ of her supply of peaches. They started with 12 bags of peaches, and Lewis sold 8 of them.

1 Lewis said to Maria, "Eight bags is $\frac{8}{12}$ of the 12 bags you wanted to sell. I think $\frac{2}{3}$ is the same as $\frac{8}{12}$. I can show you why." Lewis made this drawing. Did Lewis earn his pay? Explain your answer.

Yes. Each $\frac{1}{3}$ is the same size

$\frac{3}{3} \cdot \frac{4}{4} = \frac{8}{12}$

$\frac{1}{3}$				$\frac{1}{3}$				$\frac{1}{3}$			
$\frac{1}{12}$	$\frac{1}{12}$	$\frac{1}{12}$	$\frac{1}{12}$	$\frac{1}{12}$	$\frac{1}{12}$	$\frac{1}{12}$	$\frac{1}{12}$	$\frac{1}{12}$	$\frac{1}{12}$	$\frac{1}{12}$	$\frac{1}{12}$

$$\frac{2}{3} = \frac{8}{12}$$

Two fractions that represent the same part of a whole are **equivalent fractions**. The fractions $\frac{2}{3}$ and $\frac{8}{12}$ are equivalent.

2 Maria said, "You are just fracturing each third into 4 twelfths. You can show what you did using numbers." Here's what Maria wrote:

$$\frac{2}{3} = \frac{2 \times 4}{3 \times 4} = \frac{8}{12}$$

Discuss what Maria did. How does multiplying the numerator and denominator by 4 affect the fraction?

By multiplying 16 × 14 each unit fraction get smaller.

© Houghton Mifflin Harcourt Publishing Company

Use Fraction Bars to Find Equivalent Fractions

3 How do these fraction bars show equivalent fractions for $\frac{1}{3}$?

The numerator goes up by one & The denominator increases by 3

| $\frac{1}{3}$ | $\frac{1}{3}$ | $\frac{1}{3}$ |

| $\frac{1}{6}$ | $\frac{1}{6}$ | $\frac{1}{6}$ | $\frac{1}{6}$ | $\frac{1}{6}$ | $\frac{1}{6}$ |

| $\frac{1}{9}$ | $\frac{1}{9}$ | $\frac{1}{9}$ | $\frac{1}{9}$ | $\frac{1}{9}$ | $\frac{1}{9}$ | $\frac{1}{9}$ | $\frac{1}{9}$ | $\frac{1}{9}$ |

| $\frac{1}{12}$ | $\frac{1}{12}$ | $\frac{1}{12}$ | $\frac{1}{12}$ | $\frac{1}{12}$ | $\frac{1}{12}$ | $\frac{1}{12}$ | $\frac{1}{12}$ | $\frac{1}{12}$ | $\frac{1}{12}$ | $\frac{1}{12}$ | $\frac{1}{12}$ |

| $\frac{1}{15}$ | $\frac{1}{15}$ | $\frac{1}{15}$ | $\frac{1}{15}$ | $\frac{1}{15}$ | $\frac{1}{15}$ | $\frac{1}{15}$ | $\frac{1}{15}$ | $\frac{1}{15}$ | $\frac{1}{15}$ | $\frac{1}{15}$ | $\frac{1}{15}$ | $\frac{1}{15}$ | $\frac{1}{15}$ | $\frac{1}{15}$ |

| $\frac{1}{18}$ | $\frac{1}{18}$ | $\frac{1}{18}$ | $\frac{1}{18}$ | $\frac{1}{18}$ | $\frac{1}{18}$ | $\frac{1}{18}$ | $\frac{1}{18}$ | $\frac{1}{18}$ | $\frac{1}{18}$ | $\frac{1}{18}$ | $\frac{1}{18}$ | $\frac{1}{18}$ | $\frac{1}{18}$ | $\frac{1}{18}$ | $\frac{1}{18}$ | $\frac{1}{18}$ | $\frac{1}{18}$ |

4 You can show how to find fractions equivalent to $\frac{1}{3}$ numerically. Fill in the blanks and finish the equations. Then explain how these fraction equations show equivalent fractions.

2 equal parts	3 equal parts	4 equal parts	5 equal parts	6 equal parts
× 2	× 3	× 4	× 5	× 6
$\frac{1 \times 2}{3 \times 2} = \frac{2}{6}$	$\frac{1 \times 3}{3 \times 3} = \frac{3}{9}$	$\frac{1 \times 4}{3 \times 4} = \frac{4}{12}$	$\frac{1 \times 5}{3 \times 5} = \frac{5}{15}$	$\frac{1 \times 6}{3 \times 6} = \frac{6}{18}$

5 Tell whether the fractions are equivalent.

a. $\frac{1}{6}$ and $\frac{2}{12}$ _Yes_

b. $\frac{3}{6}$ and $\frac{5}{9}$ _No_

c. $\frac{6}{12}$ and $\frac{8}{15}$ _No_

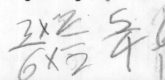

Equivalent Fractions Using Multiplication

Name _____

Use a Multiplication Table to Find Equivalent Fractions

The table on the right shows part of the multiplication table at the left. You can find fractions equivalent to $\frac{1}{3}$ by using the products in the rows for the factors 1 and 3.

×	1	2	3	4	5	6	7	8	9	10
1	1	2	3	4	5	6	7	8	9	10
2	2	4	6	8	10	12	14	16	18	20
3	3	6	9	12	15	18	21	24	27	30
4	4	8	12	16	20	24	28	32	36	40
5	5	10	15	20	25	30	35	40	45	50
6	6	12	18	24	30	36	42	48	54	60
7	7	14	21	28	35	42	49	56	63	70
8	8	16	24	32	40	48	56	64	72	80
9	9	18	27	36	45	54	63	72	81	90
10	10	20	30	40	50	60	70	80	90	100

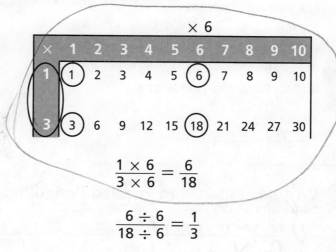

$\times 6$

×	1	2	3	4	5	6	7	8	9	10
1	1	2	3	4	5	6	7	8	9	10
3	3	6	9	12	15	18	21	24	27	30

$$\frac{1 \times 6}{3 \times 6} = \frac{6}{18}$$

$$\frac{6 \div 6}{18 \div 6} = \frac{1}{3}$$

$\frac{1}{3}$	$\frac{1}{3}$	$\frac{1}{3}$

$\frac{1}{18}$	$\frac{1}{18}$	$\frac{1}{18}$	$\frac{1}{18}$	$\frac{1}{18}$	$\frac{1}{18}$	$\frac{1}{18}$	$\frac{1}{18}$	$\frac{1}{18}$	$\frac{1}{18}$	$\frac{1}{18}$	$\frac{1}{18}$	$\frac{1}{18}$	$\frac{1}{18}$	$\frac{1}{18}$	$\frac{1}{18}$	$\frac{1}{18}$	$\frac{1}{18}$

Complete each fraction equation. Look in the top row of the table above to find the multiplier.

6 $\dfrac{1 \times 4}{3 \times 4} = \dfrac{4}{12}$

7 $\dfrac{1 \times 9}{3 \times 9} = \dfrac{9}{27}$

8 $\dfrac{1 \times 2}{3 \times 2} = \dfrac{2}{6}$

9 $\dfrac{1 \times 3}{4 \times 3} = \dfrac{3}{12}$

10 $\dfrac{3 \times 10}{10 \times 10} = \dfrac{30}{100}$

11 $\dfrac{5 \times 6}{8 \times 6} = \dfrac{30}{48}$

12 Tell whether the fractions are equivalent.

a. $\frac{3}{4}$ and $\frac{12}{16}$ ___Yes___

b. $\frac{1}{2}$ and $\frac{5}{12}$ ___No___

c. $\frac{9}{10}$ and $\frac{90}{100}$ ___Yes___

Equivalent Fractions Using Multiplication **309**

What's the Error?

Dear Students,

I tried to find a fraction equivalent to $\frac{2}{3}$.
Here's what I wrote.

$$\frac{2}{3} = \frac{5}{6}$$

Is my answer correct? If not, please help me
understand why it is wrong.

Thank you.
Puzzled Penguin

13 Write a response to Puzzled Penguin.

Your answer is incorrect.
if you mult. 3 × 2 = 6 the
2 × 2 = 4 not 5

Practice

Find a fraction equivalent to the given fraction.

14 $\frac{1}{4}$ $\frac{1 \times 2}{4 \times 2} = \frac{2}{8}$

15 $\frac{3}{8}$ $\frac{3 \times 3}{8 \times 3} = \frac{9}{24}$

16 $\frac{3}{10}$ $\frac{3}{10} \times \frac{6}{6} = \frac{18}{60}$

17 $\frac{3}{4}$ $\frac{3}{4} \times \frac{3}{3} = \frac{9}{12}$

18 $\frac{4}{5}$ $\frac{4}{5} \times \frac{7}{7} = \frac{28}{20}$

19 $\frac{7}{12}$ $\frac{7}{12} \times \frac{3}{3} = \frac{21}{36}$

20 $\frac{5}{6}$ $\frac{5}{6} \times \frac{8}{8} = \frac{40}{48} =$

21 $\frac{7}{8}$ $\frac{7}{8} \times \frac{2}{2} = \frac{14}{16}$

✓ Check Understanding

Write two fractions with the denominator 20:
one equivalent to $\frac{1}{4}$ and one equivalent to $\frac{7}{10}$.

Equivalent Fractions Using Multiplication

Name _____

Simplify Fractions

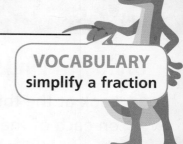

Maria had 12 boxes of apricots. She sold 10 of the boxes. Then Maria said that she sold $\frac{5}{6}$ of the boxes. She made this drawing to show that $\frac{10}{12}$ and $\frac{5}{6}$ are equivalent fractions.

| $\frac{1}{12}$ | $\frac{1}{12}$ | $\frac{1}{12}$ | $\frac{1}{12}$ | $\frac{1}{12}$ | $\frac{1}{12}$ | $\frac{1}{12}$ | $\frac{1}{12}$ | $\frac{1}{12}$ | $\frac{1}{12}$ | $\frac{1}{12}$ | $\frac{1}{12}$ |

12

| $\frac{1}{6}$ | $\frac{1}{6}$ | $\frac{1}{6}$ | $\frac{1}{6}$ | $\frac{1}{6}$ | $\frac{1}{6}$ |

1 Do you agree that $\frac{10}{12}$ and $\frac{5}{6}$ are equivalent? Why?

Yes, because $\frac{5}{6} \times \frac{2}{2} = \frac{10}{12}$

2 Maria formed groups of twelfths to get a greater unit fraction. What is that unit fraction?

$\frac{1}{6}$ $\frac{2}{12} \div \frac{2}{2} = \frac{1}{6}$

3 How many twelfths did she put in each group? In other words, what was the group size? __2__

4 Show how you can find the equivalent fraction by dividing the numerator and denominator by the group size.

$\frac{10}{12} = \frac{10 \div \boxed{2}}{12 \div \boxed{2}} = \frac{\boxed{5}}{\boxed{6}}$

To **simplify a fraction**, divide the numerator and denominator of a fraction by the same number to make an equivalent fraction made from fewer but larger unit fractions.

Use what you know to simplify each fraction to make an equivalent fraction with a unit fraction of $\frac{1}{6}$.

5 $\frac{8}{12} = \frac{8 \div \boxed{2}}{12 \div \boxed{2}} = \frac{\boxed{4}}{6}$

6 $\frac{14}{12} = \frac{14 \div \boxed{2}}{12 \div \boxed{2}} = \frac{\boxed{7}}{6} = \boxed{1}\frac{\boxed{1}}{6}$

Divide to Find Equivalent Fractions

7 Look at the thirds bar. Circle enough unit fractions on each of the other bars to equal $\frac{1}{3}$.

| $\frac{1}{18}$ | $\frac{1}{18}$ | $\frac{1}{18}$ | $\frac{1}{18}$ | $\frac{1}{18}$ | $\frac{1}{18}$ | $\frac{1}{18}$ | $\frac{1}{18}$ | $\frac{1}{18}$ | $\frac{1}{18}$ | $\frac{1}{18}$ | $\frac{1}{18}$ | $\frac{1}{18}$ | $\frac{1}{18}$ | $\frac{1}{18}$ | $\frac{1}{18}$ | $\frac{1}{18}$ | $\frac{1}{18}$ |

| $\frac{1}{15}$ | $\frac{1}{15}$ | $\frac{1}{15}$ | $\frac{1}{15}$ | $\frac{1}{15}$ | $\frac{1}{15}$ | $\frac{1}{15}$ | $\frac{1}{15}$ | $\frac{1}{15}$ | $\frac{1}{15}$ | $\frac{1}{15}$ | $\frac{1}{15}$ | $\frac{1}{15}$ | $\frac{1}{15}$ | $\frac{1}{15}$ |

| $\frac{1}{12}$ | $\frac{1}{12}$ | $\frac{1}{12}$ | $\frac{1}{12}$ | $\frac{1}{12}$ | $\frac{1}{12}$ | $\frac{1}{12}$ | $\frac{1}{12}$ | $\frac{1}{12}$ | $\frac{1}{12}$ | $\frac{1}{12}$ | $\frac{1}{12}$ |

| $\frac{1}{9}$ | $\frac{1}{9}$ | $\frac{1}{9}$ | $\frac{1}{9}$ | $\frac{1}{9}$ | $\frac{1}{9}$ | $\frac{1}{9}$ | $\frac{1}{9}$ | $\frac{1}{9}$ |

| $\frac{1}{6}$ | $\frac{1}{6}$ | $\frac{1}{6}$ | $\frac{1}{6}$ | $\frac{1}{6}$ | $\frac{1}{6}$ |

| $\frac{1}{3}$ | $\frac{1}{3}$ | $\frac{1}{3}$ |

8 Discuss how the parts of the fraction bars you circled show this chain of equivalent fractions. Explain how each different group of unit fractions is equal to $\frac{1}{3}$.

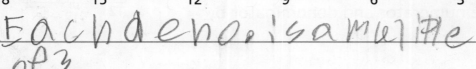

$$\frac{6}{18} = \frac{5}{15} = \frac{4}{12} = \frac{3}{9} = \frac{2}{6} = \frac{1}{3}$$

Each deno. is a mutiple
of 3.

9 Write the group size for each fraction in the chain of equivalent fractions. The first one is done for you.

6   5   4   3   2   1

10 Complete each equation by showing how you use group size to simplify. The first one is done for you.

$$\frac{6 \div 6}{18 \div 6} = \frac{1}{3} \qquad \frac{5 \div \boxed{5}}{15 \div \boxed{5}} = \frac{1}{3} \qquad \frac{4 \div \boxed{4}}{12 \div \boxed{4}} = \frac{1}{3}$$

$$\frac{3 \div \boxed{3}}{9 \div \boxed{3}} = \frac{1}{3} \qquad \frac{2 \div \boxed{2}}{6 \div \boxed{2}} = \frac{1}{3}$$

Equivalent Fractions Using Division

Name _____

Use a Multiplication Table to Find Equivalent Fractions

Multiplication table rows show relationships among equivalent fractions.

11 In Lesson 4, you used multiplication to find equivalent fractions by moving from left to right on the multiplication table. What happens to the fractions as you move from left to right? How does the size of the unit fraction change? How does the number of unit fractions change?

The numerator & denom. increased. The unit Fraction decreases. The number of unit Fractions increases

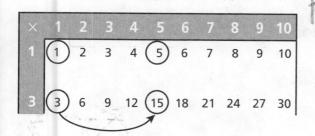

Unsimplify a fraction.

$$\frac{1}{3} = \frac{1 \times 5}{3 \times 5} = \frac{5}{15}$$

12 You can also make equivalent fractions using division by simplifying when you move from right to left on the multiplication table. What happens to the fractions as you move from right to left? How does the size of the unit fraction change? How does the number of unit fractions change?

The fractions decreased. The size of the unit fraction increases

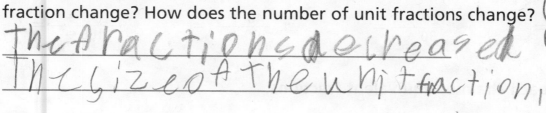

Simplify a fraction.

$$\frac{5}{15} = \frac{5 \div 5}{15 \div 5} = \frac{1}{3}$$

Use a Multiplication Table to Find Equivalent Fractions (continued)

Here are two more rows from the multiplication table moved together. These rows can be used to generate a chain of fractions equivalent to $\frac{4}{8}$.

×	1	2	3	4	5	6	7	8	9	10
4	4	8	12	16	20	24	28	32	36	40
8	8	16	24	32	40	48	56	64	72	80

Complete each equation.

13. $\frac{4 \times 6}{8 \times 6} = \frac{24}{48}$

14. $\frac{4 \times 10}{8 \times 10} = \frac{40}{80}$

15. $\frac{20 \div 5}{40 \div 5} = \frac{4}{8}$

16. $\frac{36 \div 9}{72 \div 9} = \frac{4}{8}$

17. $\frac{12 \div 3}{24 \div 3} = \frac{4}{8}$

18. $\frac{24 \div 6}{48 \div 6} = \frac{4}{8}$

Complete each chain of equivalent fractions.

19. $\frac{1}{2} = \frac{2}{2} = \frac{2 \times 4}{4} = \frac{4}{8}$

20. $\frac{7}{5} = \frac{14}{10} = \frac{28}{20}$

21. $\frac{6}{3} = \frac{8}{6} = \frac{16}{12}$

22. $\frac{4}{2} = \frac{8}{4} = \frac{16}{8}$

Practice Simplifying Fractions

Simplify each fraction.

23. $\frac{8 \div 2}{10 \div 2} = \frac{4}{5}$

24. $\frac{6 \div}{8 \div} =$

25. $\frac{15 \div}{40 \div} =$

26. $\frac{10 \div}{12 \div} =$

27. $\frac{8 \div 4}{12 \div 4} = \frac{2}{3}$

28. $\frac{20 \div}{30 \div} =$

29. $\frac{40 \div}{100 \div} =$

30. $\frac{75 \div}{100 \div} =$

Complete each chain of equivalent fractions.

31. $\frac{16}{8} = \frac{}{4} = \frac{}{2}$

32. $\frac{}{20} = \frac{1}{10} = \frac{}{5}$

33. $\frac{}{12} = \frac{}{6} = \frac{}{3}$

34. $\frac{}{8} = \frac{}{4} = \frac{}{2}$

✓ Check Understanding

Explain why equivalent fractions are the same size even though the number and size of the parts differ.

Equivalent Fractions Using Division

Name _____

Compare Fractions Using Fraction Strips and Number Lines

1 Use the number lines to compare the fractions $\frac{4}{5}$ and $\frac{7}{10}$.

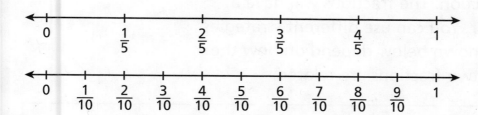

_____

2 Use the fraction strips to compare the fractions $\frac{3}{4}$ and $\frac{4}{6}$.

$\frac{1}{4}$	$\frac{1}{4}$	$\frac{1}{4}$	$\frac{1}{4}$

$\frac{1}{6}$	$\frac{1}{6}$	$\frac{1}{6}$	$\frac{1}{6}$	$\frac{1}{6}$	$\frac{1}{6}$

$\frac{1}{12}$	$\frac{1}{12}$	$\frac{1}{12}$	$\frac{1}{12}$	$\frac{1}{12}$	$\frac{1}{12}$	$\frac{1}{12}$	$\frac{1}{12}$	$\frac{1}{12}$	$\frac{1}{12}$	$\frac{1}{12}$	$\frac{1}{12}$

_____

Compare. Write >, <, or =.

3 $\frac{3}{4} \bigcirc \frac{7}{12}$

4 $\frac{3}{5} \bigcirc \frac{7}{12}$

5 $\frac{3}{5} \bigcirc \frac{6}{10}$

6 $\frac{2}{5} \bigcirc \frac{3}{6}$

7 $\frac{4}{10} \bigcirc \frac{1}{5}$

8 $\frac{2}{10} \bigcirc \frac{3}{8}$

Compare Fractions Using Common Denominators

You can compare two fractions with different denominators by writing equivalent fractions that use the same unit fraction. The fractions will have a **common denominator**. You can use different strategies to do this. The ones shown below depend on how the denominators of the two fractions are related.

Case 1: One denominator is a factor of the other. **Possible Strategy:** Use the greater denominator as the common denominator.	**Example** Compare $\frac{3}{5}$ and $\frac{5}{10}$. Use 10 as the common denominator. $\frac{3 \times 2}{5 \times 2} = \frac{6}{10}$ $\frac{6}{10} > \frac{5}{10}$, so $\frac{3}{5} > \frac{5}{10}$.
Case 2: The only number that is a factor of both denominators is 1. **Possible Strategy:** Use the product of the denominators as the common denominator.	**Example** Compare $\frac{5}{8}$ and $\frac{4}{5}$. Use 5×8, or 40, as the common denominator. $\frac{5 \times 5}{8 \times 5} = \frac{25}{40}$ $\qquad$ $\frac{4 \times 8}{5 \times 8} = \frac{32}{40}$ $\frac{25}{40} < \frac{32}{40}$, so $\frac{5}{8} < \frac{4}{5}$.
Case 3: There is a factor of both denominators that is not 1 and is not one of the denominators. **Possible Strategy:** Use a common denominator that is less than the product of the denominators.	**Example** Compare $\frac{5}{8}$ and $\frac{7}{12}$. 24 is a common multiple of 8 and 12. Use 24 as the common denominator. $\frac{5 \times 3}{8 \times 3} = \frac{15}{24}$ $\qquad$ $\frac{7 \times 2}{12 \times 2} = \frac{14}{24}$ $\frac{15}{24} > \frac{14}{24}$, so $\frac{5}{8} > \frac{7}{12}$.

Compare. Write >, <, or =.

9 $\frac{3}{5} \bigcirc \frac{2}{3}$

10 $\frac{10}{12} \bigcirc \frac{5}{6}$

11 $\frac{3}{4} \bigcirc \frac{8}{10}$

12 $\frac{4}{5} \bigcirc \frac{75}{100}$

13 $\frac{5}{8} \bigcirc \frac{3}{5}$

14 $\frac{2}{3} \bigcirc \frac{7}{10}$

Compare Fractions with Unlike Denominators

Name _____

What's the Error?

Dear Math Students,

My brother had a bowl of cherries to share.
My brother ate $\frac{3}{8}$ of the cherries. I ate $\frac{2}{5}$ of the cherries.
I wrote two fractions with a common denominator and
compared them.

$$\frac{3}{8 \times 5} = \frac{3}{40} \text{ and } \frac{2}{5 \times 8} = \frac{2}{40}$$

$$\frac{3}{40} > \frac{2}{40}, \text{ so } \frac{3}{8} > \frac{2}{5}.$$

I don't think my brother was fair. He had more than
I did! Do you agree?

Your friend,
Puzzled Penguin

15 Write a response to Puzzled Penguin.

_____

_____

_____

_____

Practice

Compare.

16 $\frac{3}{6} \bigcirc \frac{5}{10}$

17 $\frac{10}{12} \bigcirc \frac{7}{8}$

18 $\frac{2}{6} \bigcirc \frac{1}{5}$

19 $\frac{3}{8} \bigcirc \frac{1}{4}$

20 $\frac{3}{10} \bigcirc \frac{25}{100}$

21 $\frac{6}{12} \bigcirc \frac{2}{3}$

22 $\frac{2}{5} \bigcirc \frac{35}{100}$

23 $\frac{5}{12} \bigcirc \frac{9}{10}$

24 $\frac{45}{100} \bigcirc \frac{5}{10}$

25 $\frac{4}{5} \bigcirc \frac{11}{12}$

26 $\frac{3}{12} \bigcirc \frac{6}{8}$

27 $\frac{11}{12} \bigcirc \frac{9}{10}$

Compare Fractions with Unlike Denominators **317**

Practice (continued)

Solve.

Show your work.

28 Alexi and Kirsti are painting a fence around their garden. Alexi has painted $\frac{3}{8}$ of the fence. Kirsti has painted $\frac{5}{12}$ of the fence. Who has painted more of the fence?

_____

29 Esther and Lavinia have the same math homework. Esther has finished $\frac{7}{8}$ of the homework. Lavinia has finished $\frac{3}{5}$ of the homework. Who has finished more of the homework?

_____

30 Avram and Anton live on the same street. Avram's house is $\frac{3}{4}$ mile from the school. Anton's house is $\frac{7}{10}$ mile from the school. Which boy's house is a greater distance from the school?

_____

31 Leola is reading a book. On Friday, she read $\frac{25}{100}$ of the book. On Saturday, she read $\frac{3}{8}$ of the book. On which day did she read more of the book?

_____

Adding Fractions

Add.

32 $\frac{2}{10} + \frac{3}{100} =$ _____

33 $\frac{17}{100} + \frac{7}{10} =$ _____

34 $\frac{9}{10} + \frac{33}{100} =$ _____

Check Understanding

Explain how to compare the fractions $\frac{7}{12}$ and $\frac{3}{8}$.

Compare Fractions with Unlike Denominators

Use Line Plots to Solve Problems

A line plot is a graph that shows data using a number line. Mateo wants to bake raisin bread. He has several recipes that each make one loaf of bread. The line plot shows the numbers of cups of sugar in the recipes.

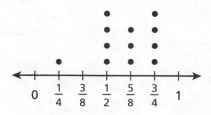

Cups of Sugar

1 How many recipes for raisin bread does Mateo have?

_____

2 How many of the recipes have more than $\frac{1}{2}$ cup of sugar?

_____

3 What is the least amount of sugar in any recipe?

_____

4 How much less sugar is in a recipe with the least sugar than in a recipe with the most sugar?

_____

5 Mateo wants to try all the recipes with exactly $\frac{5}{8}$ cup of sugar. How much sugar does he need?

_____

6 How much sugar would you expect a recipe for raisin bread to need? Explain your thinking.

_____

_____

Make a Line Plot

Mai cut up strips of color paper to make a collage. The lengths of the unused pieces are shown in the table.

Length (in inches)	Number of Pieces
$\frac{1}{2}$	4
$\frac{5}{8}$	2
$\frac{3}{4}$	2
$\frac{7}{8}$	3
$1\frac{1}{4}$	2

7 Make a line plot to display the data.

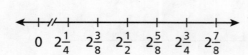

Paper Lengths (in inches)

8 Mai placed the shortest pieces in a row end to end.

How long was the row? _____

A group of students measured the widths of their hands. The measurements are shown in the table.

Width (in inches)	Number of Students
$2\frac{1}{4}$	1
$2\frac{3}{8}$	2
$2\frac{1}{2}$	2
$2\frac{5}{8}$	4
$2\frac{3}{4}$	2
$2\frac{7}{8}$	1

9 Make a line plot to display the data.

Hand Width (in inches)

10 What is the difference between the width of the widest hand and the most common hand width? _____

11 Write a problem you could solve by using the line plot.

_____

_____

✔ **Check Understanding**

Describe the parts of a line plot.

_____

Fractions and Line Plots

1   Write 5 fractions that are equivalent to $\frac{1}{4}$.

_____

2   Simplify the fraction.

$\frac{10}{25}$ = _____

3   Use the fraction strips to compare the fractions $\frac{5}{8}$ and $\frac{7}{12}$.
    Write a true statement using one of the symbols >, <, or =.

$\frac{1}{8}$	$\frac{1}{8}$	$\frac{1}{8}$	$\frac{1}{8}$	$\frac{1}{8}$	$\frac{1}{8}$	$\frac{1}{8}$	$\frac{1}{8}$

$\frac{1}{12}$	$\frac{1}{12}$	$\frac{1}{12}$	$\frac{1}{12}$	$\frac{1}{12}$	$\frac{1}{12}$	$\frac{1}{12}$	$\frac{1}{12}$	$\frac{1}{12}$	$\frac{1}{12}$	$\frac{1}{12}$	$\frac{1}{12}$

_____

Show your work.

4   Ethan plans for $\frac{3}{10}$ of the plants in his garden to be
    tomatoes. He wants $\frac{2}{5}$ of the plants to be peppers.
    Will Ethan plant more tomato plants or pepper plants?

_____

5   The line plot shows the numbers of cups of cornmeal
    used in different cornbread recipes.

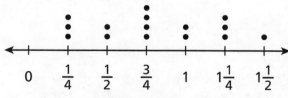

Cups of Cornmeal

How much less cornmeal is in a recipe with the least
cornmeal than in a recipe with the most cornmeal?

_____

Name _____ Date _____

Add or subtract.

1
```
  112
+ 465
```

2
```
  412
- 381
```

3
```
  7,387
+   372
```

4
```
  543,582
- 451,866
```

5
```
  34,985
+  9,077
```

6
```
  60,056
- 34,163
```

7
```
  8,309
+ 6,582
```

8
```
  6,478
- 5,116
```

9
```
  745
+ 619
```

10
```
  799
- 476
```

11
```
  31,178
-  8,636
```

12
```
  4,708
- 3,647
```

13
```
  55,268
+ 27,654
```

14
```
  487,692
+ 369,045
```

15
```
  805,245
-  27,716
```

Dear Family:

In Lessons 8 through 13 of Unit 7 of *Math Expressions*, your child will be introduced to decimal numbers. Students will begin by using what they already know about pennies, dimes, and dollars to see connections between fractions and decimals.

Students will explore decimal numbers by using bars divided into tenths and hundredths. They will relate decimals to fractions, which are also used to represent parts of a whole.

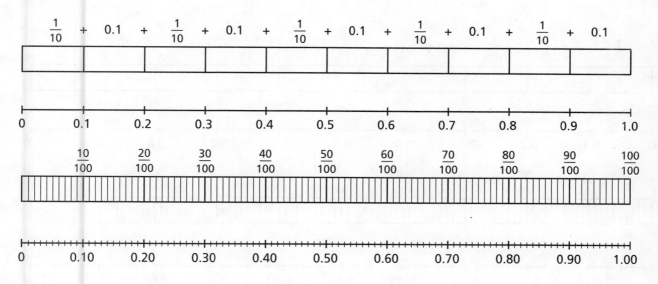

Students will read, write, and model decimal numbers. They will also learn to combine whole numbers with decimals. They will work with numbers such as 1.72 and 12.9. Students will also compare decimal numbers with other decimal numbers.

Students will apply their understanding of decimal concepts when they compare decimals.

Comparing Decimals

6.8 ◯ 3.42   6.80 ⊘ 3.42

Adding a zero makes the numbers easier to compare.

Please contact me if you have any questions or comments.

Thank you.

Sincerely,
Your child's teacher

© Houghton Mifflin Harcourt Publishing Company

CC SS Unit 7 addresses the following standards from the Common Core State Standards for Mathematics: **4.NF.A.1, 4.NF.A.2, 4.NF.C.5, 4.NF.C.6, 4.NF.C.7, 4.MD.A.2, 4.MD.B.4, and all** Mathematical Practices.

Estimada familia:

En las Lecciones 8 a 13 de la Unidad 7 de Expresiones en matemáticas, se presentarán los números decimales. Para comenzar, los estudiantes usarán lo que ya saben acerca de las monedas de un centavo, de las monedas de diez y de los dólares, para ver cómo se relacionan las fracciones y los decimales.

Los estudiantes estudiarán los números decimales usando barras divididas en décimos y centésimos. Relacionarán los decimales con las fracciones que también se usan para representar partes del entero.

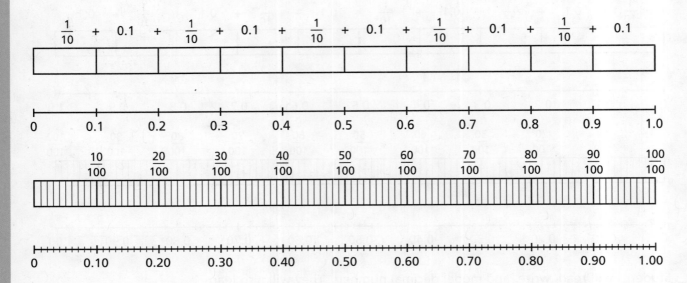

Los estudiantes leerán, escribirán y representarán números decimales. También aprenderán a combinar números enteros con decimales. Trabajarán con números tales como 1.72 y 12.9. Compararán números decimales con otros números decimales.

Al comparar decimales, los estudiantes aplicarán los conceptos decimales que ya conozcan.

Comparar decimales

6.8 ◯ 3.42   6.80 ⊚> 3.42

Añadir un cero facilita la comparación de números.

Si tiene alguna duda o algún comentario, por favor comuníquese conmigo.

Gracias.

Atentamente,
El maestro de su niño

CC SS En la Unidad 7 se aplican los siguientes estándares de los Estándares estatales comunes de matemáticas: **4.NF.A.1, 4.NF.A.2, 4.NF.C.5, 4.NF.C.6, 4.NF.C.7, 4.MD.A.2, 4.MD.B.4 y todos los de** Prácticas matemáticas.

Tenths and Hundredths

Pennies and dimes can help you understand tenths and hundredths. Discuss what you see.

100 pennies = 10 dimes = 1 dollar

100 pennies = 1 dollar   10 dimes = 1 dollar

1 penny is $\frac{1}{100}$ of a dollar   1 dime is $\frac{1}{10}$ of a dollar

1 1 penny = $\frac{1}{100}$ = 0.01

$\frac{10}{100}$ 10 of 100 equal parts

$\frac{1}{10}$ 1 of 10 equal parts

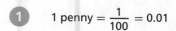

0.1
0.10

2 1 dime = $\frac{1}{10}$ = 0.1

$\frac{10}{100} + \frac{10}{100} = \frac{20}{100}$

$\frac{1}{10} + \frac{1}{10} = \frac{2}{10}$

0.1 + 0.1 = 0.2
0.10 + 0.10 = 0.20

3 $\frac{10}{100} + \frac{10}{100} + \frac{5}{100} = \frac{25}{100}$

$\frac{1}{10} + \frac{1}{10} + \frac{5}{100} = \frac{25}{100}$

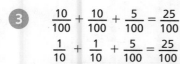

0.1 + 0.1 + 0.05 = 0.25
0.10 + 0.10 + 0.05 = 0.25

4 $\frac{25}{100} + \frac{25}{100} + \frac{25}{100} = \frac{75}{100}$

0.25 + 0.25 + 0.25 = 0.75

5 $\frac{1}{10} + \frac{1}{10} + \frac{1}{10} + \frac{1}{10} + \frac{1}{10} = \frac{5}{10} = \frac{1}{2}$

0.1 + 0.1 + 0.1 + 0.1 + 0.1 = 0.5
0.10 + 0.10 + 0.10 + 0.10 + 0.10 = 0.50

Halves and Fourths

Equal shares of 1 whole can be written as a fraction or as a decimal. Each whole dollar below is equal to 100 pennies. Discuss the patterns you see.

---

6 1 of 2 equal parts

$\frac{1}{2}$

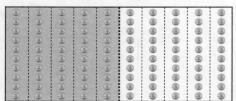

$0.5 = \frac{5}{10}$

$0.50 = \frac{50}{100}$

7 2 of 2 equal parts = 1 whole

$\frac{1}{2} + \frac{1}{2} = \frac{2}{2}$

$0.5 + 0.5 = 1.00 = \frac{5}{10} + \frac{5}{10} = \frac{10}{10}$

$0.50 + 0.50 = 1.00 = \frac{50}{100} + \frac{50}{100} = \frac{100}{100}$

---

8 1 of 4 equal parts

$\frac{1}{4}$

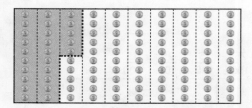

0.25

$\frac{25}{100}$

9 2 of 4 equal parts

$\frac{1}{4} + \frac{1}{4} = \frac{2}{4}$

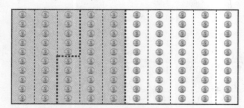

$0.25 + 0.25 = 0.50$

$\frac{25}{100} + \frac{25}{100} = \frac{50}{100}$

---

10 3 of 4 equal parts

$\frac{1}{4} + \frac{1}{4} + \frac{1}{4} = \frac{3}{4}$

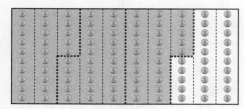

$0.25 + 0.25 + 0.25 = 0.75$

$\frac{25}{100} + \frac{25}{100} + \frac{25}{100} = \frac{75}{100}$

11 4 of 4 equal parts = 1 whole

$\frac{1}{4} + \frac{1}{4} + \frac{1}{4} + \frac{1}{4} = \frac{4}{4}$

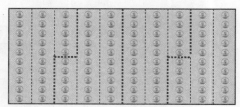

$0.25 + 0.25 + 0.25 + 0.25 = 1.00$

$\frac{25}{100} + \frac{25}{100} + \frac{25}{100} + \frac{25}{100} = \frac{100}{100}$

Relate Fractions and Decimals

Name _____

Numbers Greater Than 1

Numbers greater than 1 can be written as fractions, decimals, or mixed numbers. A mixed number is a number that is represented by a whole number and a fraction.

Discuss the patterns you see in the equivalent fractions, decimals, and mixed numbers shown below.

12 5 of 4 equal parts $= 1\frac{1}{4}$

$$\frac{1}{4} + \frac{1}{4} + \frac{1}{4} + \frac{1}{4} + \frac{1}{4} = \frac{5}{4}$$

 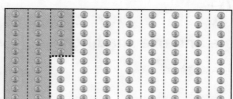

$\frac{4}{4} + \frac{1}{4}$

$$0.25 + 0.25 + 0.25 + 0.25 + 0.25 = 1.25$$

$$\frac{25}{100} + \frac{25}{100} + \frac{25}{100} + \frac{25}{100} + \frac{25}{100} = \frac{125}{100} = 1\frac{25}{100}$$

13 6 of 4 equal parts $= 1\frac{2}{4}$

$$\frac{1}{4} + \frac{1}{4} + \frac{1}{4} + \frac{1}{4} + \frac{1}{4} + \frac{1}{4} = \frac{6}{4}$$

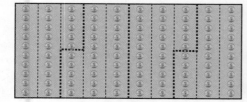 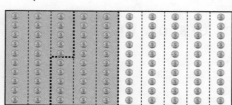

$\frac{4}{4} + \frac{2}{4}$

$$0.25 + 0.25 + 0.25 + 0.25 + 0.25 + 0.25 = 1.50$$

$$\frac{25}{100} + \frac{25}{100} + \frac{25}{100} + \frac{25}{100} + \frac{25}{100} + \frac{25}{100} = \frac{150}{100} = \frac{100}{100} + \frac{50}{100} = 1 + \frac{50}{100} = 1\frac{50}{100}$$

14 7 of 4 equal parts $= 1\frac{3}{4}$

$$\frac{1}{4} + \frac{1}{4} + \frac{1}{4} + \frac{1}{4} + \frac{1}{4} + \frac{1}{4} + \frac{1}{4} = \frac{7}{4}$$

 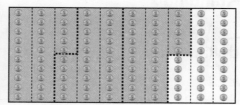

$\frac{4}{4} + \frac{3}{4}$

$$0.25 + 0.25 + 0.25 + 0.25 + 0.25 + 0.25 + 0.25 = 1.75$$

$$\frac{25}{100} + \frac{25}{100} + \frac{25}{100} + \frac{25}{100} + \frac{25}{100} + \frac{25}{100} + \frac{25}{100} = \frac{175}{100} = \frac{100}{100} + \frac{75}{100} = 1 + \frac{75}{100} = 1\frac{75}{100}$$

Relate Fractions and Decimals **327**

Model Equivalent Fractions and Decimals

Write a fraction and a decimal to represent the shaded part of each whole.

15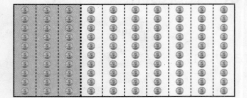

16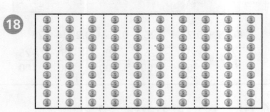

_____   _____

Divide each whole and use shading to show the given fraction or decimal.

17 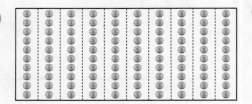   0.75

18     $\dfrac{9}{10}$

Shade these grids to show that $\dfrac{3}{2} = 1\dfrac{1}{2}$.

19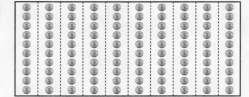

✓**Check Understanding**

Name a fraction and a decimal that represents 60 cents as part of 1 dollar. Draw a diagram to support your answer.

_____

Relate Fractions and Decimals

Name _____

Understand Tenths and Hundredths

VOCABULARY
tenth
hundredth
decimal number

Answer the questions about the bars and number lines below.

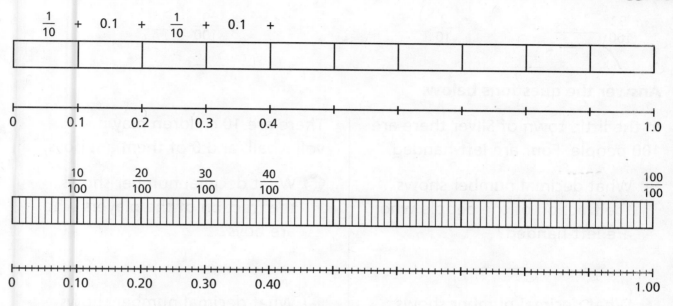

$\frac{1}{10}$ + 0.1 + $\frac{1}{10}$ + 0.1 +

0   0.1   0.2   0.3   0.4   1.0

$\frac{10}{100}$ $\frac{20}{100}$ $\frac{30}{100}$ $\frac{40}{100}$ $\frac{100}{100}$

0   0.10   0.20   0.30   0.40   1.00

1 The bars show **tenths** and **hundredths**. Finish labeling the bars and number lines using fractions and **decimal numbers**.

2 Use what you know about fractions and about money (a dime = one tenth of a dollar and a penny = one hundredth of a dollar) to explain why 3 tenths is the same as 30 hundredths.

_____

_____

_____

3 One tenth is greater than one hundredth even though 10 is less than 100. Explain why this is true.

_____

_____

Practice Writing Decimal Numbers

Write these numbers in decimal form.

4 8 tenths _____

5 6 hundredths _____

6 35 hundredths _____

7 $\frac{92}{100}$ _____

8 $\frac{2}{10}$ _____

9 $\frac{9}{100}$ _____

Answer the questions below.

In the little town of Silver there are 100 people. Four are left-handed.

10 What decimal number shows the fraction of the people who are left-handed?

_____

11 What decimal number shows the fraction of the people who are right-handed?

_____

There are 10 children playing volleyball, and 6 of them are boys.

12 What decimal number shows the fraction of the players who are boys?

_____

13 What decimal number shows the fraction of the players who are girls?

_____

Complete the table.

	Name of Coin	Fraction of a Dollar	Decimal Part of a Dollar
14	Penny	$\frac{}{100}$	
15	Nickel	$\frac{}{100} =$	
16	Dime	$\frac{}{100} =$	
17	Quarter	$\frac{}{100} =$	

✓ **Check Understanding**

Explain why 0.7 = 0.70.

Explore Decimal Numbers

0.1	0.01
0.1	**0.01**
0.2	0.02
0.2	**0.02**
0.3	0.03
0.3	**0.03**
0.4	0.04
0.4	**0.04**
0.5	0.05
0.5	**0.05**
0.6	0.06
0.6	**0.06**
0.7	0.07
0.7	**0.07**
0.8	0.08
0.8	**0.08**
0.9	0.09
0.9	**0.09**

Decimal Secret Code Cards **330A**

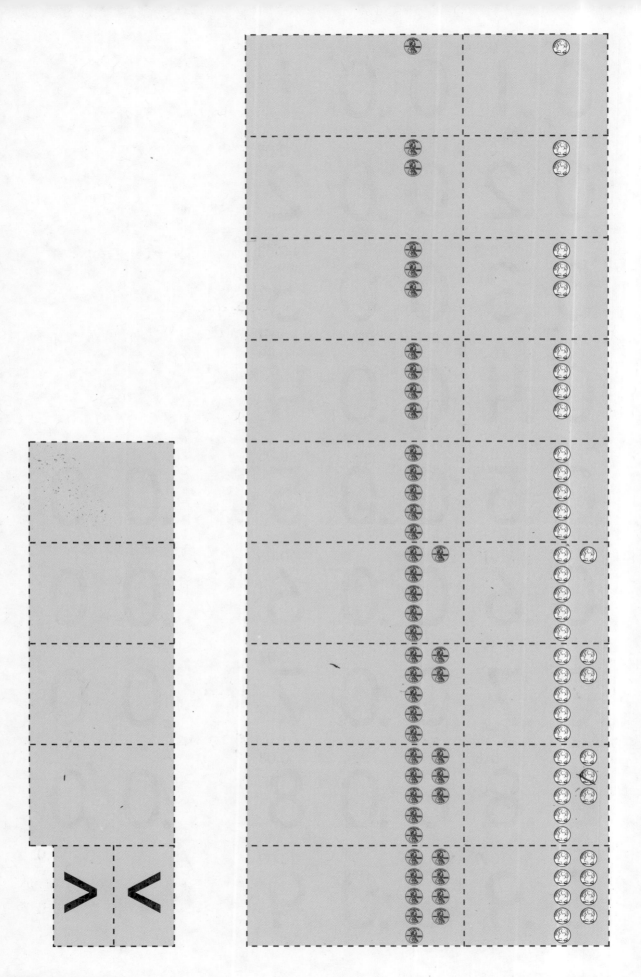

Decimal Secret Code Cards

Write Decimal Numbers

Write a decimal number to represent the distance each person has traveled.

1 Aki has traveled 3 tenths of the distance, and Steven has traveled 5 tenths of the distance.

Aki $\frac{3}{10}$ 0.3   Steven $\frac{5}{10}$ 0.5

2 José has traveled 25 hundredths of the distance, and Lakisha has traveled 18 hundredths of the distance.

José $\frac{25}{100}$ = 0.25   Lakisha $\frac{18}{100}$ = 0.18

3 Yasir has traveled 7 tenths of the distance, and Danielle has traveled 59 hundredths of the distance.

Yasir $\frac{7}{10}$ 0.7   Danielle $\frac{59}{100}$ = 0.59

4 Lea has traveled 8 hundredths of the distance, and Kwang-Sun has traveled 6 tenths of the distance.

Lea $\frac{8}{100}$ = 0.08   Kwang-Sun $\frac{6}{10}$ 0.6

Practice Comparing

Write >, <, or = to compare these numbers.

5 0.4 ⊘ 0.04   **6** 0.30 = 0.3   **7** 0.7 ⊘ 0.24   **8** 0.1 < 0.8

9 0.61 < 0.8   **10** 0.54 > 0.2   **11** 0.11 < 0.15   **12** 0.02 < 0.2

13 0.5 = 0.50   **14** 0.77 ⊘ 0.3   **15** 0.06 < 0.6   **16** 0.9 > 0.35

17 0.4 < 0.7   **18** 0.1 = 0.10   **19** 0.5 < 0.81   **20** 0.41 > 0.39

21 0.9 > 0.09   **22** 0.48 < 0.6   **23** 0.53 > 0.4   **24** 0.70 = 0.7

© Houghton Mifflin Harcourt Publishing Company

Word Problems With Decimal Numbers

Solve.

Carlos has been vacationing for one week of his 10-day vacation.

25 What decimal number represents the part of his vacation that is past? $\frac{7}{10} = 0.7$

26 What decimal number represents the part of his vacation that remains? $\frac{3}{10} = 0.3$

0.75 0.05

Jeremy spent 3 quarters and 1 nickel at the school bookstore.

27 What decimal part of a dollar did he spend? 0.80

28 What decimal part of a dollar did he not spend? 0.20

Dana is planning to run 1 tenth of a mile every day for 8 days.

29 What is the total distance she will run in 8 days? _____

30 If Dana runs 1 tenth of a mile each day for two more days, what will be the total distance she runs over the 10 days? $\frac{10}{10} = 1$ miles

Practice Writing Decimal Numbers

Write the word name of each number.

31 0.1 one tenth

32 0.73 seventy three hundredths

33 0.09 nine hundredths

34 0.5 five tenths

Write a decimal number for each word name.

35 fourteen hundredths 0.14

36 two tenths 0.2

37 eight tenths 0.8

38 six hundredths 0.06

✓ **Check Understanding**

Explain why 0.8 > 0.5 using one or more of the methods taught in this lesson.

Compare Decimals to Hundredths

Name _____

Discuss Symmetry Around the Ones

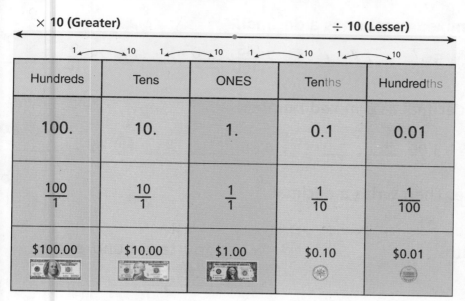

× 10 (Greater) ← → ÷ 10 (Lesser)

Hundreds	Tens	ONES	Tenths	Hundredths
100.	10.	1.	0.1	0.01
$\frac{100}{1}$	$\frac{10}{1}$	$\frac{1}{1}$	$\frac{1}{10}$	$\frac{1}{100}$
$100.00	$10.00	$1.00	$0.10	$0.01

1 Discuss symmetries and relationships you see in the place value chart.

2 Is it easier to see place value patterns in **a** or **b**? Discuss why.

a. 500 50 5 .5 .05

b. 500 50 5 0.5 0.05

Show and Read Decimal Numbers

Use your Decimal Secret Code Cards to make numbers on the frame.

Place value	Hundreds	Tens	ONES	Tenths	Hundredths
Make numbers					
Read numbers			•	and tenths	hundredths

© Houghton Mifflin Harcourt Publishing Company

Write Numbers in Decimal Form

Read and write each mixed number as a decimal.

3 $3\frac{1}{10}$ _3.1_   **4** $5\frac{7}{100}$ _5.07_   **5** $2\frac{46}{100}$ _2.049_   **6** $28\frac{9}{10}$ _29.9_

Read and write each decimal as a mixed number.

7 12.8 _$12\frac{8}{10}$_   **8** 3.05 _$3\frac{5}{100}$_   **9** 4.85 _$4\frac{85}{100}$_   **10** 49.7 _$49\frac{7}{10}$_

Read each word name. Then write a decimal for each word name.

11 sixty-one hundredths

$\frac{61}{100} = 0.61$

12 six and fourteen hundredths

$6\frac{14}{100} = 6.14$

13 seventy and eight tenths

$70\frac{8}{10} = 70.8$

14 fifty-five and six hundredths

$55\frac{6}{100}$ 55.06

Expanded Form

Write each decimal in expanded form.

15 8.2 _8 + 0.2_

16 17.45 _10 + 7 + 0.4 + 0.05_

17 106.24 _100 + 6 + 0.2 + 0.04_

18 50.77 _50 + 0.7 + 0.07_

19 312.09 _300 + 10 + 2 + 0.09_

20 693.24 _600 + 9 + 3 + 0.20 + 0.04_

Solve.

21 There are 100 centimeters in 1 meter. A snake crawls 3 meters and 12 more centimeters. What decimal represents the number of meters the snake crawls?

_____

22 There are 100 pennies in 1 dollar. A jar contains 20 dollars. You add 8 pennies to the jar. What decimal represents the number of dollars in the jar?

_____

✓ **Check Understanding**

Describe how each place value in a decimal number is related to the place value to its left and to the place value to its right.

Decimals Greater Than 1

100	10	1
1 0 0	1 0	1
200	20	2
2 0 0	2 0	2
300	30	3
3 0 0	3 0	3
400	40	4
4 0 0	4 0	4
500	50	5
5 0 0	5 0	5
600	60	6
6 0 0	6 0	6
700	70	7
7 0 0	7 0	7
800	80	8
8 0 0	8 0	8
900	90	9
9 0 0	9 0	9

Decimal Secret Code Cards

| $1 | $10 | $100 |

| $1 | $10 | $100 |
| $1 | $10 | $100 |

$1	$10	$100
$1	$10	$100
$1	$10	$100

$1	$10	$100
$1	$10	$100
$1	$10	$100
$1	$10	$100

$1	$10	$100
$1	$10	$100
$1	$10	$100
$1	$10	$100
$1	$10	$100

$1	$1	$10	$10	$100	$100
$1		$10		$100	
$1		$10		$100	
$1		$10		$100	
$1		$10		$100	

$1	$1	$10	$10	$100	$100
$1	$1	$10	$10	$100	$100
$1		$10		$100	
$1		$10		$100	
$1		$10		$100	

$1	$1	$10	$10	$100	$100
$1	$1	$10	$10	$100	$100
$1	$1	$10	$10	$100	$100
$1.		$10		$100	
$1		$10		$100	

$1	$1	$10	$10	$100	$100
$1	$1	$10	$10	$100	$100
$1	$1	$10	$10	$100	$100
$1	$1	$10	$10	$100	$100
$1		$10		$100	

Name _____

Zeros in Greater Decimal Numbers

Use the tables to answer Problems 1–4.

1 What happens if we insert a zero to the right of a whole number?

_____

Insert Zeros to the Right			
Whole Numbers		**Decimal Numbers**	
3	30	0.3	0.30
67	670	6.7	6.70

2 What happens if we insert a zero to the right of a decimal number?

_____

_____

Insert Zeros to the Left			
Whole Numbers		**Decimal Numbers**	
3	03	0.3	0.03
67	067	6.7	6.07

3 What happens if we insert a zero to the left of a whole number?

_____

4 What happens if we insert a zero to the left of a decimal number just after the decimal point?

_____

_____

5 Are whole numbers and decimal numbers alike or different when it comes to putting in extra zeros? Explain your answer.

_____

_____

_____

6 Do the pairs of numbers below have the same value? Why or why not?

0.6 and .6 _____   .25 and 0.25 _____   0.9 and 0.90 _____

_____

Compare Decimals

You can use your understanding of place value and the placement
of zeros in decimal numbers to compare decimal numbers.

Problem:	Solution:
Which of these numbers is the greatest: 2.35, 2.3, or 2.4?	2.35 With the places aligned and 2.30 the extra zeros added, we 2.40 can see which is greatest.

Write >, <, or = to compare these numbers.

7 27.5 ◯ 8.37　　**8** 6.04 ◯ 5.98　　**9** 7.36 ◯ 7.38　　**10** 36.9 ◯ 37.8

11 0.5 ◯ 0.26　　**12** 0.09 ◯ 0.9　　**13** 0.8 ◯ 0.80　　**14** 0.42 ◯ 0.6

Use the table to answer Problems 15 and 16.

15 Francis measured some common insects.
The table shows the lengths in centimeters.
List the insects from longest to shortest.

Lengths of Insects	
Name	**Length**
Ladybug	0.64 cm
Moth	0.3 cm
Mosquito	0.32 cm
Cricket	1.8 cm
Bumblebee	2 cm

_____ _____ _____ _____ _____

　Longest　　　　　　　　　　　　　　　　　Shortest

16 Maya read about a stick insect that is 1.16 centimeters long.
She compared the length with the lengths in the table.
Maya says the mosquito is longer than the stick insect because
0.32 > 0.16. Is Maya's reasoning correct? Explain.

_____

✓ **Check Understanding**

Write >, <, or = to compare these numbers.

20.7 ◯ 20.07

　　　　　　　Compare Decimals Greater Than 1

Math and Autumn Leaves

The weather in different parts of the United States has a noticeable effect on plants and trees. In warm parts of the country, trees can keep their leaves all year long. In the northern states, fall weather causes leaves to change color. People from around the country plan trips to see and photograph the red, yellow, orange, and brown leaves. A fall leaf-viewing trip could involve driving through a national forest, biking along a rail trail, or hiking into the mountains.

Solve.

Show your work.

1   One popular park for photographing leaves in autumn is Macedonia Brook State Park in Kent, Connecticut. The Yellow Trail is the shortest hiking trail and is $\frac{51}{100}$ mile long. What is this fraction written as a decimal?

2   The Rogers family is visiting Massachusetts to see the leaves change color. The Old Eastern Marsh Trail is $1\frac{2}{5}$ miles long. The Bradford Rail Trail is $1\frac{3}{10}$ miles long. The Rogers family wants to take the longer trail. Which trail should they take?

 Content Standards **4.NF.A.1, 4.NF.A.2, 4.NF.C.6, 4.NF.C.7**
Mathematical Practices **MP1, MP2, MP3, MP4, MP6, MP7**

Focus on Mathematical Practices **337**

Clarkston Park

Joshua and Lily are going north to participate in a walking tour in Clarkston Park to photograph the leaves. Here is the trail map of the different walking trails.

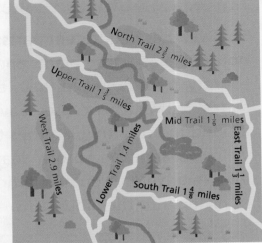

3 Write the length of the West Trail as a mixed number.

_____

4 Which trail is shorter: the West Trail or the North Trail? Write the comparison using >, <, or =.

_____

5 Write the length of the Lower Trail as a mixed number.

_____

6 Which trail is longer: the Lower Trail or the South Trail? Write the comparison using >, <, or =.

_____

7 Write a fraction that is equivalent to the length of the North Trail.

_____

8 Use the number line below and the benchmark numbers to name the trail whose length in miles is represented by each point.

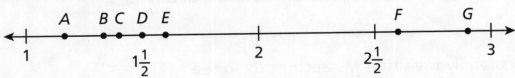

A: _____   E: _____

B: _____   F: _____

C: _____

G: _____

D: _____

Focus on Mathematical Practices

Write the correct answer.

1 Mark has 100 marbles. Eight are bumblebee marbles. What decimal number shows the fraction of marbles that are bumblebees?

_____

2 An insect egg can be as small as two hundredths of a millimeter long. What is this number written as a decimal?

_____

3 On a tree farm, 0.28 of the trees are oak. Write this decimal as a fraction.

_____

4 James ran a race in 2.2 hours. Casey ran the same race in 2.25 hours. Who took less time to run the race?

_____

5 Traci rode her mountain bike 2.8 miles on Monday. She rode 2.7 miles on Tuesday. On which day did she ride a longer distance? Write the comparison using >, <, or =.

_____

Fluency Check 20

PATH to FLUENCY

Add or subtract.

1   512
     + 436

2   38,923
     + 35,468

3   782,465
     − 447,869

4   674
     − 338

5   128,492
     + 56,932

6   2,492
     + 455

7   76,829
     + 2,457

8   32,589
     − 3,741

9   935
     + 562

10   8,241
     + 4,976

11   40,670
     − 19,843

12   9,945
     − 3,831

13   3,280
     − 1,159

14   506
     − 305

15   670,834
     − 88,560

1 For Exercises 1a–1d, write > or < to make the inequality true.

1a. $\frac{3}{5}$ ◯ $\frac{1}{5}$

1c. $\frac{9}{10}$ ◯ $\frac{9}{12}$

1b. $\frac{2}{8}$ ◯ $\frac{2}{3}$

1d. $\frac{5}{8}$ ◯ $\frac{7}{8}$

2 Choose numbers from the tiles to make an equivalent fraction with the least possible denominator.

| 2 | 3 | 4 | 6 |

$\frac{8}{12} = \dfrac{\boxed{}}{\boxed{}}$

3 Farid measures the masses of four books in kilograms. He records the data in the table. Which two books have the same mass?

Masses of Books

Book	1	2	3	4
Mass (kg)	1.12	1.20	1.02	1.2

(A) Books 1 and 3

(C) Books 3 and 4

(B) Books 2 and 3

(D) Books 2 and 4

4 In a survey, $\frac{7}{10}$ of the students said they watched the news last week. Complete the fraction equation.

$$\frac{7}{10} = \frac{\boxed{}}{100}$$

5 A trail is $\frac{7}{12}$ mile long. Select the trail length that is shorter than $\frac{7}{12}$ mile. Mark all that apply.

(A) $\frac{3}{8}$ mile   (B) $\frac{2}{3}$ mile   (C) $\frac{3}{4}$ mile   (D) $\frac{1}{2}$ mile

6 On average, a chimpanzee spends about $\frac{2}{5}$ of the day sleeping. A squirrel spends about $\frac{5}{8}$ of the day sleeping. A three-toed sloth spends about $\frac{5}{6}$ of the day sleeping. For Exercises 6a–6d, choose True or False to best describe the statement.

6a. A chimpanzee spends more of the day sleeping than a three-toed sloth.   ○ True   ○ False

6b. A squirrel spends more of the day sleeping than a chimpanzee.   ○ True   ○ False

6c. A three-toed sloth spends more of the day sleeping than a squirrel.   ○ True   ○ False

6d. A chimpanzee sleeps more than the other two types of animals.   ○ True   ○ False

7 Emily and Leah each brought a full water bottle to practice. Their bottles were the same shape, but Leah's bottle was taller than Emily's. Each girl drank $\frac{1}{2}$ of her water.

Part A

Draw a picture to show Emily and Leah's water bottles. Shade the bottles to show how much water each girl originally had. Then cross out the amount each girl drank.

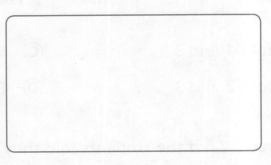

Part B

Did each girl drink the same amount of water? Explain.

8 Locate and draw a point on the number line for the fraction or mixed number. Then label it with its corresponding letter.

a. $4\frac{1}{2}$ b. $\frac{7}{8}$ c. $1\frac{3}{4}$ d. $3\frac{1}{4}$ e. $2\frac{3}{8}$

9 For Exercises 9a–9c, complete the chain of equivalent fractions.

9a. $\dfrac{2}{3} = \dfrac{\boxed{}}{6} = \dfrac{\boxed{}}{9} = \dfrac{\boxed{}}{12}$

9b. $\dfrac{6}{12} = \dfrac{\boxed{}}{6} = \dfrac{1}{\boxed{}}$

9c. $\dfrac{3}{4} = \dfrac{\boxed{}}{8} = \dfrac{9}{\boxed{}}$

10 Write five fractions that are equivalent to $\frac{1}{2}$.

11 A lizard has a length of $\frac{43}{100}$ meter. Write $\frac{43}{100}$ in decimal form.

12 Tione is researching beetles. She records the lengths of some beetles in the table.

Length (in inches)	Number of Beetles
$\frac{1}{4}$	2
$\frac{1}{2}$	3
$\frac{3}{4}$	6
1	1
$1\frac{1}{4}$	4
$1\frac{1}{2}$	2

Part A

Make a line plot to display the data.

Part B

How many beetles are less than 1 inch long? _____ beetles

13 Show how to simplify the fraction $\frac{6}{10}$. Choose numbers from the tiles to complete the fraction equation. You may use a number more than once.

2	3
5	6

$$\frac{6}{10} = \frac{6 \div \boxed{}}{10 \div \boxed{}} = \frac{\boxed{}}{\boxed{}}$$

14 Write a decimal to make the statement true.

| 0.1 | 0.3 | 0.8 |

☐ > 0.65   0.15 > ☐   ☐ = 0.30

15 A forest ranger saw 10 deer. There were 2 male and 8 female deer. What fraction or decimal number shows the part of the deer that were female? Mark all that apply.

Ⓐ $\frac{2}{10}$ Ⓒ 0.80   Ⓔ $\frac{8}{10}$

Ⓑ 0.2   Ⓓ 0.08   Ⓕ 0.8

16 Each model represents 1 whole dollar. The shaded part represents the part of a dollar Loren took to the bank.

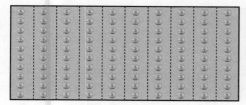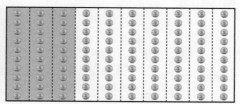

Part A

Write a mixed number to represent the part of a dollar Loren took to the bank.

Part B

Loren says she can represent the part of a dollar she took to the bank as 1.3 but not as 1.30. Do you agree? Why or why not?

17 Beth wrote the number sixty-one and twelve hundredths in decimal form.

What did Beth write? ☐

18 Trading cards come in packs of 100. Becca has 3 full packs and 7 more cards. For Exercises 18a–18d, choose Yes or No to tell whether the number represents the number of packs Becca has.

18a. 3.07   ○ Yes   ○ No

18b. 3 and 7 hundredths   ○ Yes   ○ No

18c. three and one seventh   ○ Yes   ○ No

18d. 3.7   ○ Yes   ○ No

19 A vet measures the mass of three puppies. Suzy's mass is 3.3 kilograms. Buster's mass is 3.03 kilograms, and Charlie's mass is 3.30 kilograms.

Part A
Is Suzy's mass the same as Charlie's? Explain.

Part B
A fourth puppy, Pluto, has a mass of 3.33 kilograms. Which of the four puppies has the least mass? Explain how you found your answer.

Bicycle Parking Only

Jacob rides his bike to school and parks it in the bicycle rack near the front entrance. He counted the number of bicycles in the rack each school day for a week and recorded his count in this table.

Bicycles in the Front Entrance Rack					
Day	Monday	Tuesday	Wednesday	Thursday	Friday
Number of Bicycles	3	7	4	8	10

1. The rack can hold up to 10 bicycles. What fraction of the bicycle rack was used each day?

_____

_____

2. Jenny thinks that on Tuesday, about $\frac{1}{2}$ of the bicycle rack was used. Jacob thinks about $\frac{1}{2}$ of the rack was used on Wednesday. Who is correct? Use a diagram or number line to justify your answer.

_____

_____

_____

3. What decimal number shows the part of the bicycle rack that was used each day?

_____

_____

4. Jacob thinks it is easier to write decimals than fractions to describe how much of the rack was used each day. Do you think he would feel the same if the rack had spaces for 12 bikes? Explain your reasoning.

_____

_____

_____

Jacob counted the number of bicycles at the back entrance for the same week. The back entrance bicycle rack also holds 10 bicycles. His results are in the table below.

Bicycles in the Back Entrance Rack					
Day	Monday	Tuesday	Wednesday	Thursday	Friday
Number of Bicycles	7	4	8	7	2

5 What fraction of the spaces was used in the back entrance rack on Friday?

_____

6 On which day of the week were $\frac{4}{5}$ of the spaces in the back entrance rack used? Explain how you solved the problem.

_____

_____

7 What decimal number shows the part of the back entrance rack that was not used each day?

_____

_____

_____

8 On the following Monday, $\frac{3}{5}$ of the front entrance rack was used and 0.3 of the back entrance rack was used. Were there more bikes in the front rack or the back rack? Explain.

_____

_____

_____

Dear Family:

In the first half of Unit 8, your child will be learning to recognize and describe geometric figures. One type of figure is an angle. Your child will use a protractor to find the measures of angles.

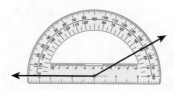

Other figures, such as triangles, may be named based on their angles and sides.

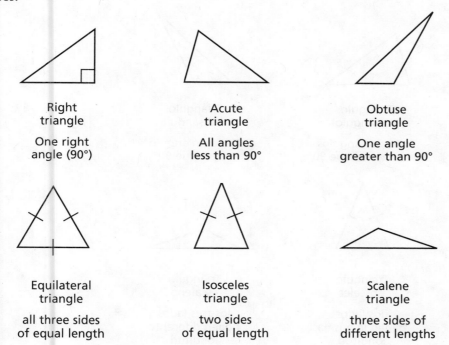

Right triangle	Acute triangle	Obtuse triangle
One right angle (90°)	All angles less than 90°	One angle greater than 90°

Equilateral triangle	Isosceles triangle	Scalene triangle
all three sides of equal length	two sides of equal length	three sides of different lengths

Be sure that your child continues to review and practice the basics of multiplication and division. A good understanding of the basics will be very important in later math courses when students learn more difficult concepts in multiplication and division.

If you have any questions or comments, please contact me.

Thank you.

Sincerely,
Your child's teacher

Unit 8 addresses the following standards from the Common Core State Standards for Mathematics: **4.MD.C.5, 4.MD.C.5.a, 4.MD.C.5.b, 4.MD.C.6, 4.MD.C.7, 4.G.A.1, 4.G.A.2, 4.G.A.3, and all** Mathematical Practices.

Estimada familia:

En la primera parte de la Unidad 8, su niño aprenderá a reconocer y a describir figuras geométricas. Un ángulo es un tipo de figura. Su niño usará un transportador para hallar las medidas de los ángulos.

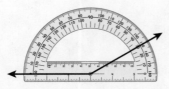

Otras figuras, tales como los triángulos, se nombran según sus ángulos y lados.

Triángulo rectángulo	**Triángulo acutángulo**	**Triángulo obtusángulo**
Tiene un ángulo recto (90°)	Todos los ángulos son menores que 90°	Tiene un ángulo mayor que 90°

Triángulo equilátero	**Triángulo isósceles**	**Triángulo escaleno**
los tres lados tienen la misma longitud	dos lados tienen la misma longitud	los tres lados tienen diferente longitud

Asegúrese de que su niño siga repasando y practicando las multiplicaciones y divisiones básicas. Es importante que domine las operaciones básicas para que, en los cursos de matemáticas de más adelante, pueda aprender conceptos de multiplicación y división más difíciles.

Si tiene alguna pregunta o algún comentario, por favor comuníquese conmigo.

Gracias.

Atentamente,
El maestro de su niño

En la Unidad 8 se aplican los siguientes estándares de los Estándares estatales comunes de matemáticas: **4.MD.C.5, 4.MD.C.5.a, 4.MD.C.5.b, 4.MD.C.6, 4.MD.C.7, 4.G.A.1, 4.G.A.2, 4.G.A.3 y todos los de** Prácticas matemáticas.

acute angle

angle

acute triangle

circle

adjacent sides

degree (°)

A figure formed by two rays with the same endpoint.

An angle smaller than a right angle.

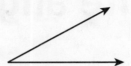

A plane figure that forms a closed path so that all the points on the path are the same distance from a point called the center.

A triangle with three acute angles.

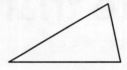

A unit for measuring angles.

Two sides that meet at a point.

Example:
Sides *a* and *b* are adjacent.

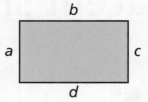

diagonal of a quadrilateral	isosceles triangle
endpoint	line
equilateral triangle	line of symmetry

A triangle with at least two sides of equal length.

A line segment that connects two opposite corners (vertices).

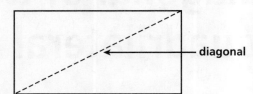

A straight path that goes on forever in opposite directions.

Example:
line *AB*

The point at either end of a line segment or the beginning point of a ray.

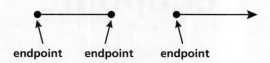

A line on which a figure can be folded so that the two halves match exactly.

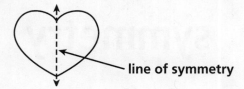

Having all sides of equal length.

Example:
An equilateral triangle

line segment

obtuse triangle

line symmetry

opposite sides

obtuse angle

parallel lines

A triangle with one obtuse angle.

Part of a line that has two endpoints.

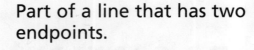

Sides that are across from each other; they do not meet at a point.

Example:

Sides *a* and *c* are opposite.

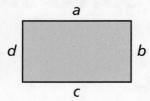

A figure has line symmetry if it can be folded along a line to create two halves that match exactly.

Lines in the same plane that never intersect are parallel. Line segments and rays that are part of parallel lines are also parallel.

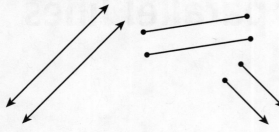

An angle greater than a right angle and less than a straight angle.

parallelogram	polygon
perpendicular lines	protractor
point	quadrilateral

A closed plane figure with sides made of straight line segments.

A quadrilateral with both pairs of opposite sides parallel.

A semicircular tool for measuring and constructing angles.

Lines, line segments, or rays are perpendicular if they form right angles.

Example:
These two lines are perpendicular.

A
|
C ←——□——→ D
|
↓
B

A polygon with four sides.

A location in a plane. It is usually shown by a dot.

ray

right angle

reflex angle

right triangle

rhombus

scalene
triangle

One of four angles made by
perpendicular line segments.

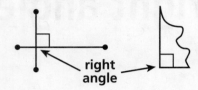

Part of a line that has
one endpoint and
extends without end in
one direction.

A triangle with one
right angle.

An angle with a measure
that is greater than 180° and
less than 360°.

A triangle with no equal
sides is a scalene triangle.

A parallelogram with sides
of equal length.

straight angle

vertex of a
polygon

trapezoid

vertex of an
angle

A point that is shared by two sides of a polygon.

vertex

An angle that measures 180°.

A quadrilateral with exactly one pair of parallel sides.

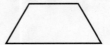

A point that is shared by two sides of an angle.

vertex

Points, Lines, and Line Segments

A **point** is shown by a dot. It is named by a capital letter.

• X

A **line** is a straight path that goes on forever in both directions. When you draw a line, you put arrows on the ends to show that it goes on and on. Lines can be named by any two points on the line. Here are $\overleftrightarrow{AB}$, $\overleftrightarrow{GK}$, and $\overleftrightarrow{PN}$.

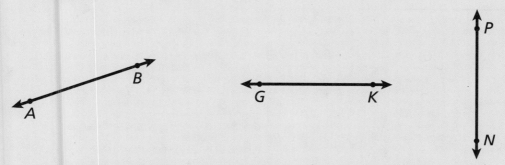

A **line segment** is part of a line. It has two ends, which are called **endpoints**. Segments are named by their endpoints. Here are $\overline{RS}$, $\overline{WT}$, and $\overline{DJ}$.

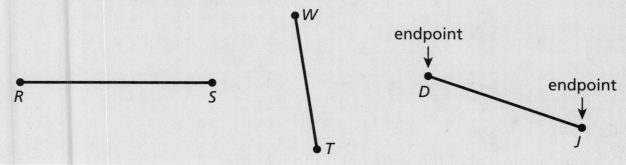

endpoint

endpoint

1. You can measure to find the length of a line segment, but you cannot measure to find the length of a line. Explain why.

_____

_____

_____

_____

Drawing Points, Rays, and Angles

VOCABULARY
angle
ray
vertex of an angle

An **angle** is formed by two **rays** with the same endpoint, called the **vertex**.

You can label figures with letters to name them. This is ∠ABC. Its rays are $\overrightarrow{BA}$ and $\overrightarrow{BC}$.

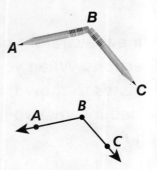

Draw and label each figure.

2 Draw and label a point. Write the name of your point. _____

3 Draw a ray. Label the endpoint. Write the name of your ray. _____

4 Draw an angle. Label the vertex and the two rays. Write the name of your angle. _____

Points, Rays, and Angles

Discuss Angles

Angles can be many different sizes.

VOCABULARY
acute angle
right angle
obtuse angle

Discuss the groups of angles.

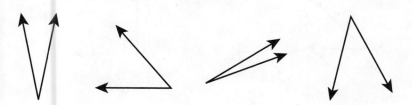

5 How are all of these **acute angles** alike?

_____

_____

6 How is an acute angle different from a **right angle**?

_____

_____

7 How are all of these **obtuse angles** alike?

_____

_____

8 How is an obtuse angle different from a right angle?

_____

_____

9 How is an obtuse angle different from an acute angle?

_____

_____

Classify Angles

Use the letters to name each angle. Then write *acute,* **right, or** *obtuse* **to describe each angle.**

10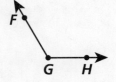

_____

_____

11

_____

_____

12

_____

_____

13 Use the letters to name two acute and two obtuse angles in this figure. Write *acute* or *obtuse* to describe each angle.

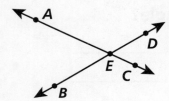

_____

_____

_____

_____

14 Draw and label a right angle, an acute angle, and an obtuse angle.

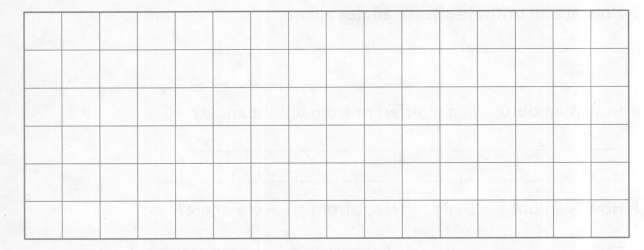

✓ **Check Understanding**

Draw and label a line, a line segment, and a ray.

Sort Angles

Cut along the dashed lines.

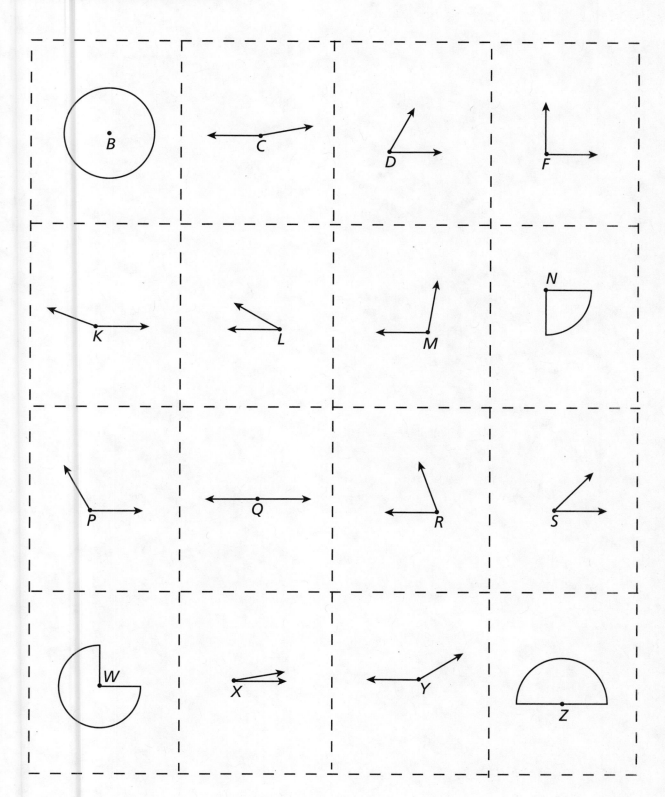

Points, Rays, and Angles

Name _____

Introduce Degrees

VOCABULARY
degree
right angle
straight angle

Angles are measured in units called **degrees**. One degree is the measure of one very small turn from one ray to the other.

This angle has a measure of 1 degree.

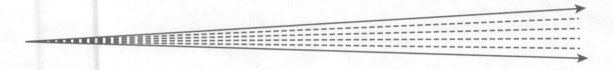

The measure of an angle is the total number of 1-degree angles that fit inside it.

This angle measures 5 degrees.

The symbol for degrees is a small raised circle (°). You can write the measure of the angle above as 5°. $5 \times 1° = 5°$

A **right angle** has a measure of 90°.
A 90° turn traces one quarter of a circle.

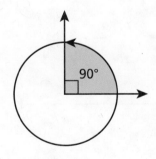

A **straight angle** measures 180°.
A 180° turn traces one half of a circle.

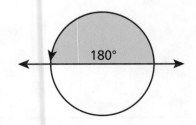

The angle below measures 360°.
A 360° turn traces a complete circle.

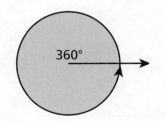

CC SS Content Standards 4.MD.C.5, 4.MD.C.5.a, 4.MD.C.5.b, 4.MD.C.6, 4.G.A.1
Mathematical Practices MP3, MP5, MP6, MP7

Measuring Angles **355**

Use a Protractor

VOCABULARY
protractor

A **protractor** is a tool that is used to measure angles in degrees. This protractor shows that ∠ABC measures 90°.

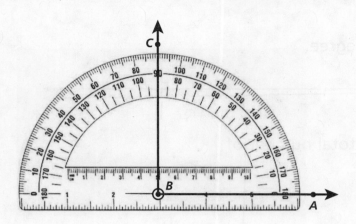

Measure each angle with your protractor. Write the measure.

1

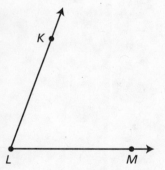

∠KLM = _____

2

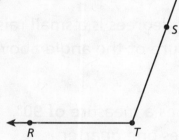

∠STR = _____

3

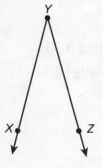

∠XYZ = _____

4

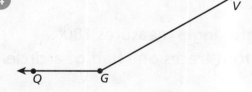

∠QGV = _____

Measuring Angles

Name _____

Sketch Angles

Sketch each angle, or draw it using a protractor.

⑤   90°

⑥   45°

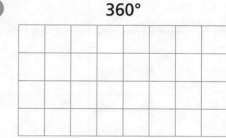

⑦   180°

⑧   360°

Use Reasoning

Use the figures at the right to answer the following questions.

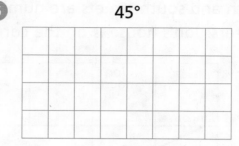

⑨ Name one right angle in each figure.

_____

⑩ Name one straight angle in each figure.

_____

⑪ How much greater is the measure of
∠KRB than the measure of ∠IAO?

_____

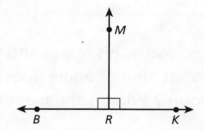

⑫ Which angle appears to be a 45° angle?

_____

⑬ The measure of ∠IAE is 135°.

What is the measure of ∠OAE? _____

What is the measure of ∠UAE? _____

Angles in the Real World

Here is a map of Jon's neighborhood. The east and west
streets are named for presidents of the United States.
The north and south streets are numbered. The avenues
have letters. Jon's house is on the corner of Lincoln and First.

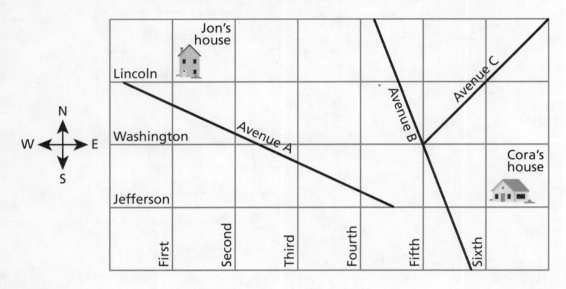

14 What do the arrows to the left of the map tell you?

_____

15 Jon leaves his house and rides his bike south on First.
What kind of angle does he make for each turn in this
route? What is the measure of each angle?

• Jon turns southeast onto Avenue A. _____

• When he reaches Washington, he turns west. _____

• When he gets back to First, he turns south. _____

16 Jon's cousin Cora leaves Jon's house and rides east on
Lincoln to Avenue B. Draw the angle Cora makes if she
turns southeast. What is the measure of the angle?

_____

✓ Check Understanding

Draw a 90° angle, a 135° angle, and a 180° angle.

Name _____

Measure Angles in a Circle

VOCABULARY
circle
reflex angle

You can show all the different types of angles in a **circle**.

Acute angle

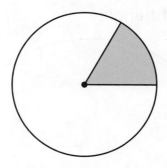

greater than 0° and less than 90°

Right angle

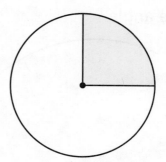

90°

Obtuse angle

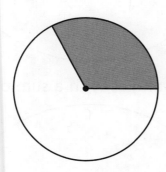

greater than 90° and less than 180°

Straight angle

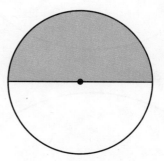

180°

Reflex angle

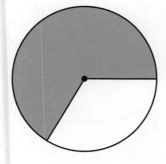

greater than 180° and less than 360°

Circle

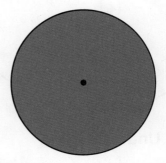

360°

CC SS Content Standards **4.MD.C.5, 4.MD.C.5.a, 4.MD.C.5.b, 4.MD.C.6, 4.MD.C.7, 4.G.A.1**
Mathematical Practices **MP2, MP3, MP6, MP8**

Draw Angles in a Circle

Use a straightedge and a protractor to draw and shade an angle of each type. Measure and label each angle.

1 obtuse angle

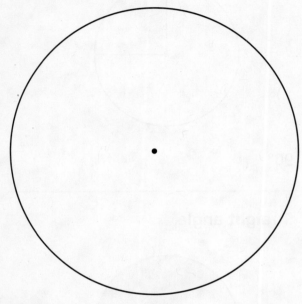

2 straight angle

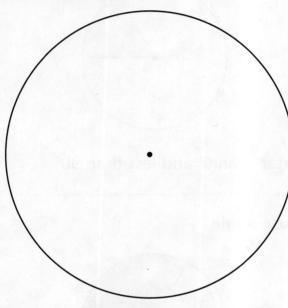

3 acute angle

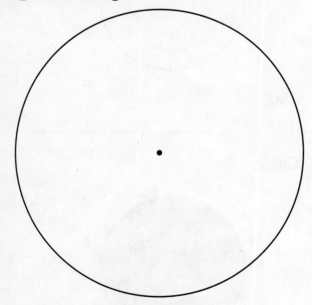

4 three angles with a sum of 360°

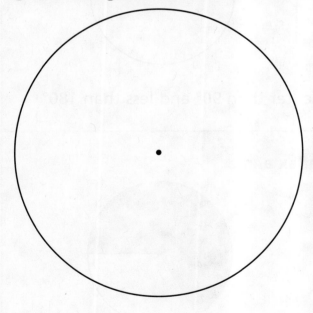

✓ **Check Understanding**

Write an addition equation that shows the sum of your angle measures in Exercise 4.

Circles and Angles

Write the correct answer.

1 Measure angle *ABC*. Tell whether it is an acute, obtuse, or right angle.

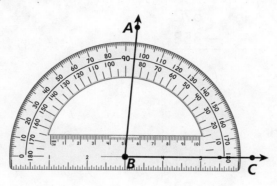

_____

2 Liam sketches a 45° angle. Circle the angle Liam sketches.

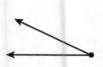   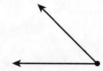

Draw the figure.

3 Ray *EF*

4 Right angle *ABC*

5 Obtuse angle *DEF*

Fluency Check 21

Name _______________ Date _______________

PATH to FLUENCY

Add or subtract.

1. $\begin{array}{r} 434 \\ +\ 315 \\ \hline \end{array}$

2. $\begin{array}{r} 572 \\ -\ 358 \\ \hline \end{array}$

3. $\begin{array}{r} 374{,}583 \\ +\ 44{,}625 \\ \hline \end{array}$

4. $\begin{array}{r} 506{,}721 \\ -\ 452{,}899 \\ \hline \end{array}$

5. $\begin{array}{r} 3{,}274 \\ +\ 835 \\ \hline \end{array}$

6. $\begin{array}{r} 30{,}430 \\ -\ 18{,}478 \\ \hline \end{array}$

7. $\begin{array}{r} 813 \\ +\ 526 \\ \hline \end{array}$

8. $\begin{array}{r} 56{,}923 \\ -\ 7{,}361 \\ \hline \end{array}$

9. $\begin{array}{r} 7{,}846 \\ -\ 2{,}515 \\ \hline \end{array}$

10. $\begin{array}{r} 676 \\ -\ 421 \\ \hline \end{array}$

11. $\begin{array}{r} 5{,}707 \\ -\ 2{,}644 \\ \hline \end{array}$

12. $\begin{array}{r} 17{,}948 \\ +\ 23{,}324 \\ \hline \end{array}$

13. $\begin{array}{r} 672{,}943 \\ -\ 45{,}867 \\ \hline \end{array}$

14. $\begin{array}{r} 4{,}839 \\ +\ 6{,}127 \\ \hline \end{array}$

15. $\begin{array}{r} 67{,}359 \\ +\ 4{,}418 \\ \hline \end{array}$

Discuss Angles of a Triangle

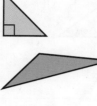

VOCABULARY
right triangle
obtuse triangle
acute triangle

The prefix *tri-* means "three," so it is easy to remember that a triangle has 3 angles. Triangles can take their names from the kind of angles they have.

- A **right triangle** has one right angle, which we show by drawing a small square at the right angle.

- An **obtuse triangle** has one obtuse angle.

- An **acute triangle** has three acute angles.

1 You can also use letters to write and talk about triangles. This triangle is △QRS. Name its three angles and their type.

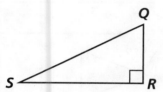

_____

_____

_____

2 What kind of triangle is △QRS? How do you know?

_____

_____

3 Draw and label a right triangle, an acute triangle, and an obtuse triangle.

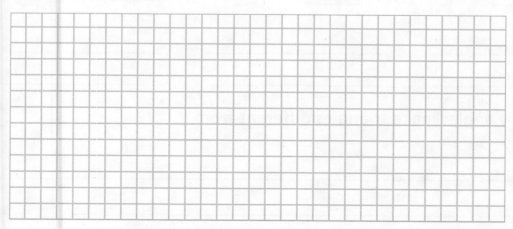

Identify Angles of a Triangle

Name each triangle by its angles. Explain your thinking.

4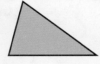

_____

_____

5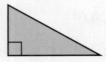

_____

_____

6

_____

_____

7

_____

_____

8

_____

_____

9

_____

_____

10

_____

_____

11

_____

_____

12

_____

_____

13

_____

_____

14

_____

_____

15

_____

_____

16 Describe how angles make triangles different from one another.

_____

_____

Name Triangles

Name _____

Discuss Sides of a Triangle

Triangles can be named by their sides. Small "tick marks" on the sides of triangles tell us when sides are equal.

• The prefix *equi-* means "equal." Triangles that have three equal sides are called **equilateral**.

• Triangles that have two equal sides are called **isosceles**. The word *isosceles* comes from very old words that mean "equal legs."

• Triangles with no equal sides are called **scalene**. All triangles that are not equilateral or isosceles are scalene.

Use these triangles to answer the questions.

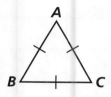
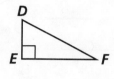
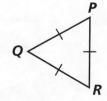
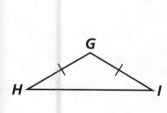
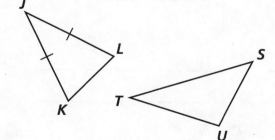

17 Write the letter names of the scalene triangles.

_____

18 Write the letter names of the equilateral triangles.

_____

19 Write the letter names of the isosceles triangles.

_____

Identify Sides of a Triangle

Name each triangle by its sides. Explain your thinking.

20

_____

_____

21

_____

_____

22

_____

_____

23

_____

_____

24

_____

_____

25

_____

_____

26

_____

_____

27

_____

_____

28

_____

_____

29

_____

_____

30

_____

_____

31

_____

_____

32 Explain how sides make triangles different from each other.

_____

_____

Name Triangles

Sort Triangles in Different Ways

33 Write a capital letter and a lowercase letter inside each triangle below, using the keys at the right.

Cut out the triangles and use the diagram below to sort them in different ways.

acute = a
obtuse = o
right = r

Isosceles = I
Scalene = S
Equilateral = E

Triangles

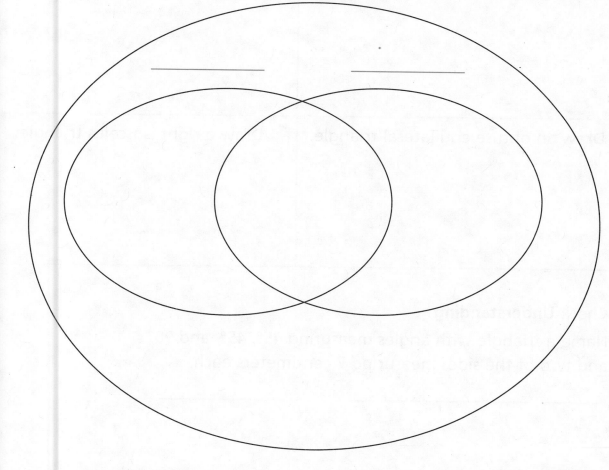

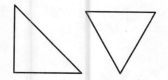 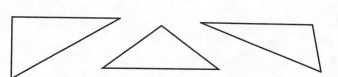

Possible Ways to Name Triangles

Draw each triangle. If you can't, explain why.

34 Draw a right scalene triangle.	**35** Draw an obtuse scalene triangle.
36 Draw a right equilateral triangle.	**37** Draw an acute isosceles triangle.
38 Draw an obtuse equilateral triangle.	**39** Draw a right isosceles triangle.

✓ **Check Understanding**

Name a triangle with angles measuring 45°, 45°, and 90° and two of the sides measuring 7 centimeters each.

Name Triangles

Name _____

Add Angle Measures

Two angles can be put together to form another angle. The measure of the whole angle is the sum of the measures of the smaller angles. The measure of the whole angle shown is 105°.

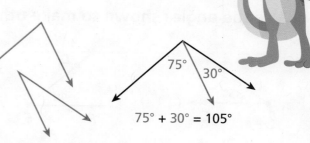

75° + 30° = 105°

What kind of angle is formed when the two angles are put together? What is its measure?

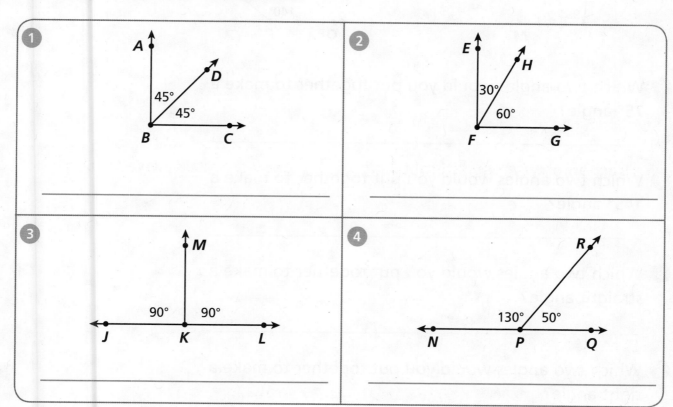

1. A, D, B, C — 45°, 45°

2. E, H, F, G — 30°, 60°

3. M, J, K, L — 90°, 90°

4. R, N, P, Q — 130°, 50°

5. An angle is made from two angles with measures 80° and 70°. Write and solve an equation to find the measure of the whole angle.

Show your work.

_____
_____
_____

CC SS Content Standards **4.MD.C.6, 4.MD.C.7, 4.G.A.1**
Mathematical Practices **MP1, MP2, MP3, MP5, MP6**

Put Angles Together

Use the angles shown to make other angles.

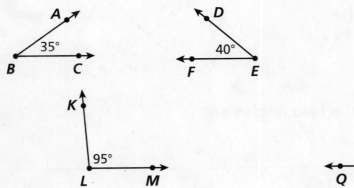

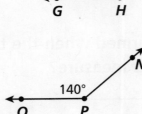

6. Which two angles would you put together to make a 75° angle?

_____

7. Which two angles would you put together to make a 145° angle?

_____

8. Which two angles would you put together to make a straight angle?

_____

9. Which two angles would you put together to make a right angle?

_____

10. If you put all five angles together, what would be the measure of the whole angle? What kind of figure would you form?

_____

11. Use a protractor and straightedge to draw the angle formed by putting ∠ABC and ∠KLM together. Show its measure.

Compose and Decompose Angles

Name _____

Subtract Angle Measures

Write an equation to find the unknown angle measure.

12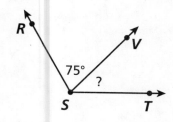

The measure of ∠RST is 120°.
What is the measure of ∠VST?

_____

_____

13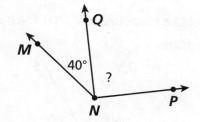

The measure of ∠MNP is 130°. What
is the measure of ∠QNP?

_____

_____

14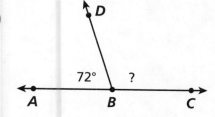

The measure of ∠ABC is 180°.
What is the measure of ∠DBC?

_____

_____

15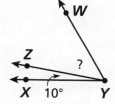

The measure of ∠XYW is 60°.
What is the measure of ∠ZYW?

_____

_____

16 Draw your own angle problem and share it with a partner.

_____

17 When a right angle is made from two smaller
angles, what must be true about the smaller angles?

_____

18 When a straight angle is made from two smaller
angles, what must be true about the smaller angles?

_____

_____

Compose and Decompose Angles **371**

What's the Error?

Dear Math Students,

I want to find the measure of ∠DBE in the
following diagram.

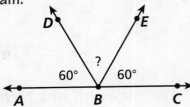

I wrote and solved this equation.

$180° - (60° + 60°) = x$

$180° - 60° + 60° = x$

$120° + 60° = x$

$180° = x$

This answer doesn't make sense.
Did I do something wrong?

Your friend,
Puzzled Penguin

19 Write a response to Puzzled Penguin.

_____

_____

_____

_____

_____

_____

 Check Understanding

Explain how to use an equation to find an unknown angle measure.

Compose and Decompose Angles

Name _____

Add Angle Measures

Use an equation to solve.

1 The ski jumper shown makes angles with her skis as shown. What is the sum of the angles?

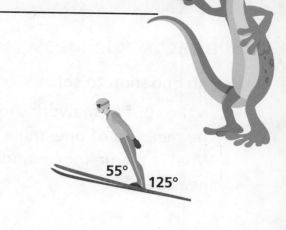

55° 125°

_____

2 In the roof framework shown, ∠ABD and ∠DBC have the same measure. What is the measure of ∠DBA? What is the measure of ∠ABC?

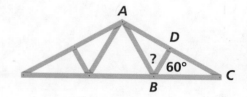

A
D
? 60°
B C

_____

3 In the simple bridge structure shown, the measure of ∠RSV is 30° and ∠VST is a right angle. What is the measure of ∠RST?

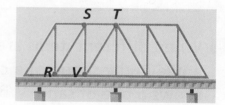

S T
R V

_____

The circle at the right represents all of the students in a class. Each section represents the students in the class who chose a certain type of animal as their favorite type of pet. The angle measures for some sections are given.

4 What is the sum of the angle measures for Cat, Dog, and Horse?

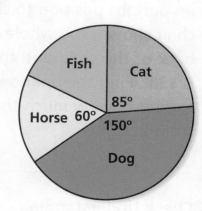

Fish
Cat
85°
Horse 60°
150°
Dog

_____

5 What is the total angle measure for the circle? What is the angle measure for Fish?

_____

Subtract Angle Measures

Use an equation to solve.

6 In the roof framework shown, the measure of one angle is 80°. What is the unknown angle measure?

_____

7 The railing on a stairway makes a 50° angle with the upright post. What is the unknown angle measure in the diagram?

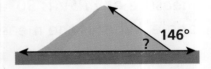

_____

8 When different items are poured, they form a pile in the shape of a cone. The diagram shows a pile of sand. What is the angle the sand makes with the ground?

_____

9 In a reclining chair, you can push back from an upright position to sit at an angle. In the chair shown, the whole angle between the back of the chair and the seat of the chair is 130°. Find the unknown angle measure to find by how much the chair is reclined from upright.

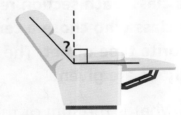

_____

✓**Check Understanding**
Give an example from your home, classroom, or neighborhood where you could use an equation to find an unknown angle measure.

_____

Real World Problems

Write the correct answer.

1 Which three angles can be put together to make a 165° angle?

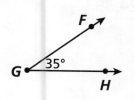

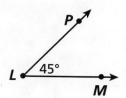

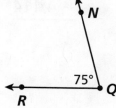

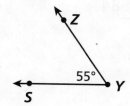

_____

2 Jeri measures one of two equal angles in the figure below. Write an addition equation to find the sum of the angles.

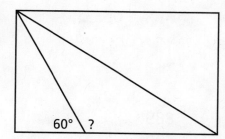

_____

3 In the window design shown, the measure of one angle is 60°. Write a subtraction equation to find the unknown angle measure.

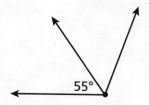

_____

Name the triangle by its angles.

4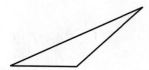

5

_____   _____

Name _____ **Date** _____

Add or subtract.

1
```
  1,573
+ 3,684
```

2
```
  6,345
- 4,114
```

3
```
  32,583
- 24,392
```

4
```
  428
+ 361
```

5
```
  719
- 483
```

6
```
  7,832
+  556
```

7
```
  78,362
+ 14,839
```

8
```
  3,450
- 2,137
```

9
```
  273
+ 825
```

10
```
  889
- 523
```

11
```
  387,387
+ 126,836
```

12
```
  20,000
-  4,357
```

13
```
  708,427
- 473,892
```

14
```
  72,497
+  3,538
```

15
```
  548,702
-  94,582
```

Dear Family:

Your child has been learning about geometry throughout this unit. In this second half of the unit, your child will be learning how to recognize and describe a group of geometric figures called quadrilaterals, which get their name because they have four (*quad-*) sides (*-lateral*). Five different kinds of quadrilaterals are shown here.

Square
4 equal sides
opposite sides parallel
4 right angles

Rectangle
2 pairs of parallel sides
4 right angles

Rhombus
4 equal sides
opposite sides parallel

Parallelogram
2 pairs of parallel sides

Trapezoid
exactly 1 pair of opposite sides parallel

If you have any questions or comments, please contact me.

Sincerely,
Your child's teacher

CC SS **Unit 8 addresses the following standards from the** Common Core State Standards for Mathematics: **4.MD.C.5, 4.MD.C.5.a, 4.MD.C.5.b, 4.MD.C.6, 4.MD.C.7, 4.G.A.1, 4.G.A.2, 4.G.A.3, and all** Mathematical Practices.

Estimada familia:

Durante esta unidad, su niño ha estado aprendiendo acerca de geometría.
En esta parte de la unidad, su niño aprenderá cómo reconocer y describir
un grupo de figuras geométricas llamadas cuadriláteros, que reciben ese
nombre porque tienen cuatro *(quadri-)* lados *(-lateris)*. Aquí se muestran
cinco tipos de cuadriláteros:

Cuadrado
4 lados iguales
lados opuestos paralelos
4 ángulos rectos

Rectángulo
2 pares de lados
paralelos
4 ángulos rectos

Rombo
4 lados iguales
lados opuestos paralelos

Paralelogramo
2 pares de lados paralelos

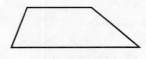

Trapecio
exactamente 1 par de lados paralelos opuestos

Si tiene alguna pregunta o algún comentario, por favor comuníquese
conmigo.

Atentamente,
El maestro de su niño

© Houghton Mifflin Harcourt Publishing Company

En la Unidad 8 se aplican los siguientes estándares de los Estándares estatales comunes de matemáticas: **4.MD.C.5, 4.MD.C.5.a,
4.MD.C.5.b, 4.MD.C.6, 4.MD.C.7, 4.G.A.1, 4.G.A.2, 4.G.A.3 y todos los de** Prácticas matemáticas.

378 UNIT 8 LESSON 7   Parallel and Perpendicular Lines and Line Segments

Name _____

Define Parallel Lines

VOCABULARY
parallel lines

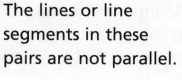

The lines or line segments in these pairs are **parallel**.

The lines or line segments in these pairs are not parallel.

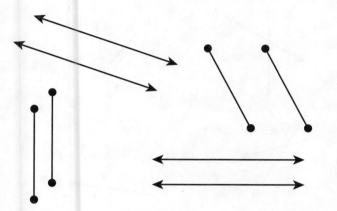

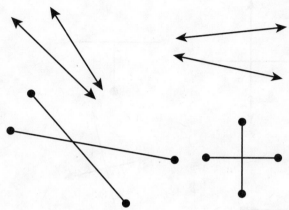

1 What do you think it means for two lines to be parallel?

_____

_____

_____

Draw Parallel Lines

2 Draw and label a pair of parallel lines.

3 Draw and label a figure with one pair of parallel line segments.

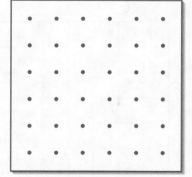

Define Perpendicular Lines

VOCABULARY
perpendicular lines

The lines or line segments in these pairs are **perpendicular**.

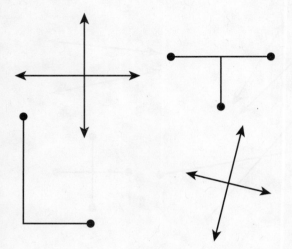

The lines or line segments in these pairs are not perpendicular.

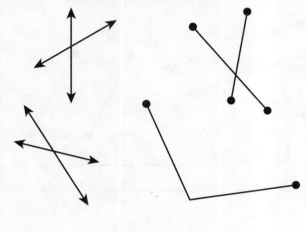

4 What do you think it means for two lines to be perpendicular?

_____

_____

_____

Draw Perpendicular Lines

5 Draw and label a pair of perpendicular lines.

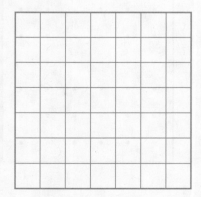

6 Draw and label a figure with one pair of perpendicular line segments.

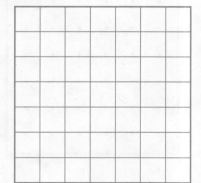

Parallel and Perpendicular Lines and Line Segments

Identify Types of Lines

Tell whether each pair of lines is *parallel, perpendicular,* or *neither*.

7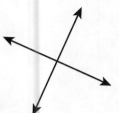

8

_____

9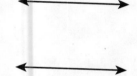

10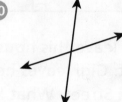

_____

11 Draw a pair of parallel line segments.

12 First, draw a line segment 3 centimeters long. Then, draw a line segment 6 centimeters long that looks perpendicular to your first line segment.

Line Segments on a Map

Use the map.

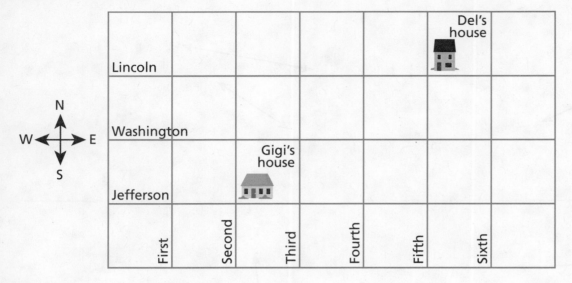

13 On Wednesday, Del leaves his house and walks West along Lincoln Street. Gigi leaves her house and walks East along Jefferson Street. What kind of line segments are Lincoln Street and Jefferson Street?

_____

14 Will Del and Gigi ever meet? If so, where?

_____

15 On Friday, Del leaves his house and walks South along Fifth Street. Gigi leaves her house and walks East along Jefferson Street. What kind of line segments are Fifth Street and Jefferson Street?

_____

16 Will Del and Gigi ever meet? If so, where?

_____

✔ **Check Understanding**

Explain how to decide whether two lines are _parallel_, _perpendicular,_ or _neither_.

Parallel and Perpendicular Lines and Line Segments

Name _____

Identify Sides of Quadrilaterals

VOCABULARY
quadrilateral
adjacent sides
opposite sides

Look at these quadrilaterals.

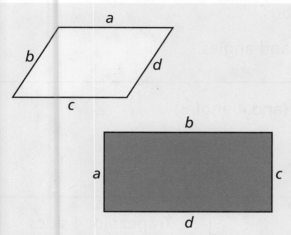
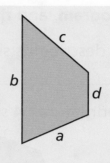
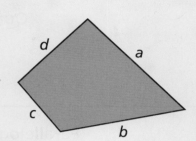

In all of the quadrilaterals, the sides labeled *a* and *b*
are **adjacent** to each other. The sides labeled *b* and *c*
are also adjacent to each other.

1 What do you think it means for two sides to be adjacent?

_____

_____

2 Which other sides are adjacent to each other?

_____

In all of the quadrilaterals, the sides labeled *a* and *c*
are **opposite** each other.

3 What do you think it means for two sides to be
opposite each other?

_____

_____

4 Which other sides are opposite each other?

_____

Identify Types of Quadrilaterals

VOCABULARY
trapezoid
parallelogram
rhombus

Some quadrilaterals are special because they have parallel sides or right angles. You already know about rectangles and squares. Other types of quadrilaterals are the **trapezoid**, **parallelogram**, and **rhombus**.

You can list each type and describe its sides and angles.

Quadrilateral: 4 sides (and 4 angles)

Parallelogram: 4 sides
2 pairs of opposite sides parallel

Trapezoid: 4 sides
exactly 1 pair of
opposite sides parallel

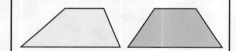

Rhombus: 4 sides
2 pairs of opposite sides
parallel
4 equal sides

Rectangle: 4 sides
2 pairs of opposite sides
parallel
4 right angles

Square: 4 sides
2 pairs of opposite sides parallel
4 right angles
4 equal sides

Classify Quadrilaterals

Name _____

Draw Special Quadrilaterals

5 Draw a quadrilateral that has exactly one pair of opposite sides parallel. What type of quadrilateral is it?

_____

6 Draw a quadrilateral that has two pairs of opposite sides parallel. What type of quadrilateral is it? Is there more than one answer?

_____

_____

7 Draw a quadrilateral that has two pairs of opposite sides parallel, 4 equal sides, and no right angles. What type of quadrilateral is it?

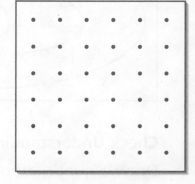

_____

Identify Relationships

Why is each statement below true?

8 A rhombus is always a parallelogram, but a parallelogram isn't always a rhombus.

_____

_____

9 A rectangle is a parallelogram, but a parallelogram is not necessarily a rectangle.

_____

_____

10 A square is a rectangle, but a rectangle does not have to be a square.

_____

_____

11 Complete the category diagram by placing each word in the best location.

Quadrilateral	Parallelogram	Rhombus
Trapezoid	Rectangle	Square

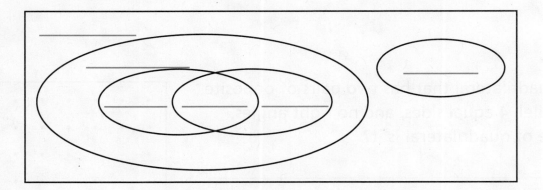

✓ Check Understanding
Draw a quadrilateral that is not a parallelogram.

Classify Quadrilaterals

Name _____

Sort and Classify Quadrilaterals

Cut along the dashed lines.

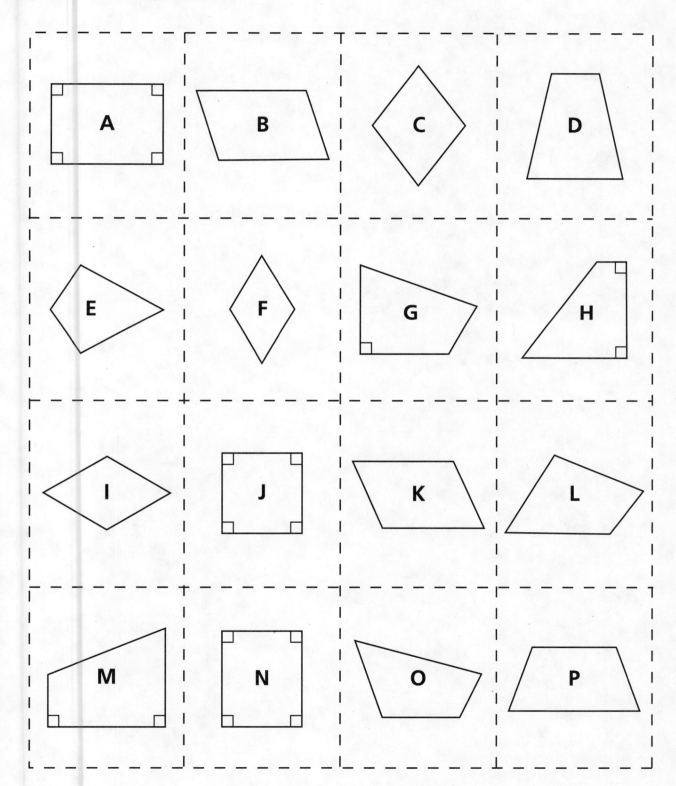

Classify Quadrilaterals **386A**

Classify Quadrilaterals

Name _____

Use Diagonals to Make Triangles

A **diagonal of a quadrilateral** is a line segment
that connects two opposite corners (vertices).
You can make triangles by drawing a diagonal
on a quadrilateral.

**List all names for each quadrilateral in Exercises 1–3.
Then use letters to name the triangles you can make with
the diagonals and tell what kind of triangles they are.**

1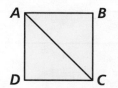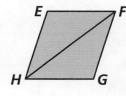

_____   _____   _____

_____   _____   _____

2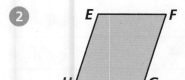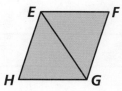

_____   _____   _____

_____   _____   _____

3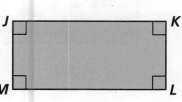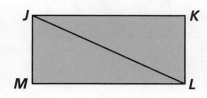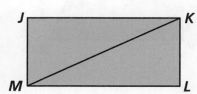

_____   _____   _____

_____   _____   _____

Content Standards 4.G.A.1, 4.G.A.2
Mathematical Practices MP3, MP5, MP6, MP7, MP8

Use Diagonals to Make Triangles (continued)

List all names for each quadrilateral in Exercises 4–6.
Then use letters to name the triangles you can make with
the diagonals and tell what kind of triangles they are.

4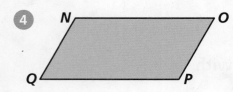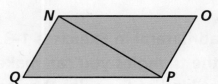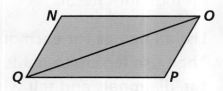

_____ _____ _____

_____ _____ _____

5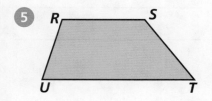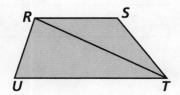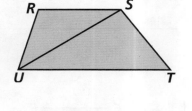

_____ _____ _____

_____ _____ _____

_____ _____ _____

6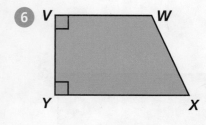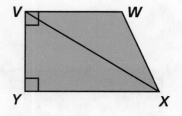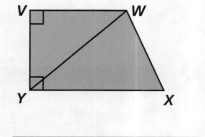

_____ _____ _____

_____ _____ _____

Decompose Quadrilaterals and Triangles

Build Quadrilaterals With Triangles

You can make a quadrilateral by joining the equal sides
of two triangles that are the same size and shape.

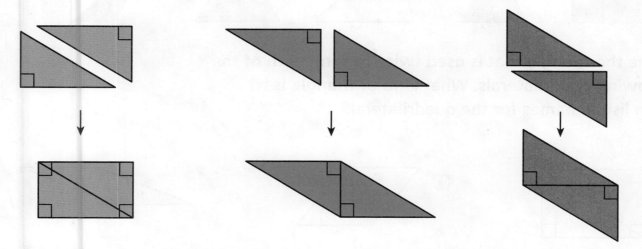

**Cut out the triangles below. For each exercise, glue two
of the triangles on this paper so that the stated sides
are joined. Then write the name of the quadrilateral.**

7 $\overline{AB}$ is joined to $\overline{AB}$ **8** $\overline{AC}$ is joined to $\overline{AC}$ **9** $\overline{BC}$ is joined to $\overline{BC}$

_____   _____   _____

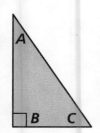
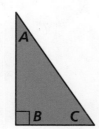
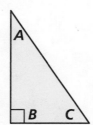
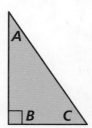
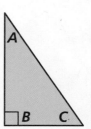
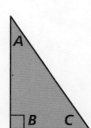

    Decompose Quadrilaterals and Triangles **389**

Match Quadrilaterals with Triangles

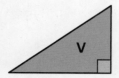 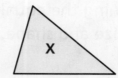

Name the triangle that is used twice to form each of the
following quadrilaterals. What kind of triangle is it?
Then list all names for the quadrilateral.

10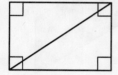

_____

_____

_____

11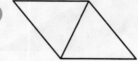

_____

_____

_____

12

_____

_____

_____

13

_____

_____

_____

14

_____

_____

_____

15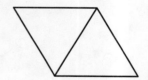

_____

_____

_____

Decompose Quadrilaterals and Triangles

Draw Perpendicular Lines in Triangles

VOCABULARY
polygon
vertex of a polygon

A **vertex** is a point shared by two sides of a **polygon**. Triangles are examples of polygons.

Draw a scalene triangle *ABC*.

16 What is true about the sides of your triangle?

_____

17 Draw a segment from one vertex so that it is perpendicular to the opposite side. Label the segment and mark the right angles.

_____

18 Name the triangles formed. What kind of triangles are they?

_____

_____

19 Are the triangles you formed the same size and shape?

_____

Draw an isosceles triangle *JKL* for Exercises 20–23.

20 What is true about the sides of your triangle?

_____

21 Draw a segment from the vertex between the equal sides of the triangle so that it is perpendicular to the opposite side. Label the segment and mark the right angles.

_____

© Houghton Mifflin Harcourt Publishing Company

Draw Perpendicular Lines in Triangles (continued)

Use your isosceles triangle *JKL* to answer the questions.

22 Name the segments formed by the perpendicular segment in △*JKL*. What is true about the lengths of the segments?

_____

_____

23 Name the triangles formed. Are they the same size and shape?

_____

What's the Error?

Dear Math Students,

I tried to do Exercises 20–23 again using an equilateral triangle PQR. I found that $\overline{PS}$ and $\overline{RS}$ that I formed are not each half the length of side $\overline{PR}$ and the new triangles are not the same size and shape.

Did I do something wrong?

Your friend,
Puzzled Penguin

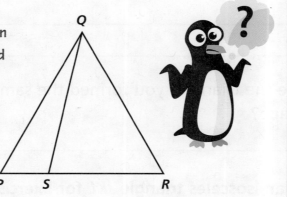

24 Write a response to Puzzled Penguin.

_____

_____

_____

_____

✓ **Check Understanding**

Complete the sentence. You can make _____ by drawing a diagonal on a quadrilateral.

Decompose Quadrilaterals and Triangles

Tell whether the lines are *parallel* or *perpendicular*.

1

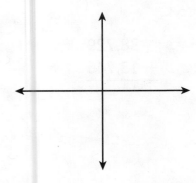

_____

2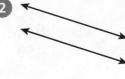

_____

3 Deena draws four line segments to make a figure. The figure has two pairs of parallel sides and no right angles. What figure does Deena draw?

_____

4 Gerard made a plaque. It has two pairs of parallel sides, all four sides are equal, and all the angles are right angles. What shape is the plaque?

_____

List all the names for the quadrilateral. Then write the type of triangles you can make with the diagonals.

5

_____

_____

Add or subtract.

1   1,846
      + 4,539

2   672
      − 459
      _227_

3   38,729
      + 13,746

(handwritten work: × 13745, 105380, 21,9 225)

4   8,695
      − 4,265

5   475,932
      − 58,484

6   70,007
      − 43,862

7   348,421
      + 74,325

8   5,016
      − 3,204

9   783
      − 411

10   209
      + 360

11   62,678
      − 3,822

12   94,327
      + 3,882

13   704,586
      − 479,219

14   5,836
      + 816

15   815
      + 934

Sort Polygons by Angles

Use these polygons for Exercises 1–5.

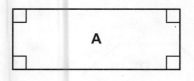
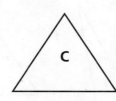
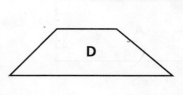
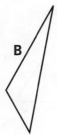

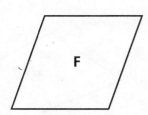
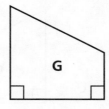
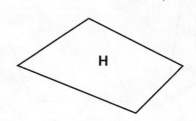

1 Which figures have one or more acute angles?

_____

2 Which figures have one or more right angles?

_____

3 Which figures have one or more obtuse angles?

_____

4 Which figures have both acute angles and right angles?

_____

5 Which figures have both acute angles and obtuse angles?

_____

Sort Polygons by Sides

Use these polygons for Exercises 6–10.

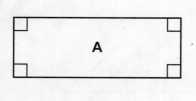
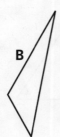
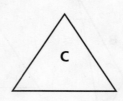
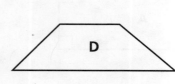

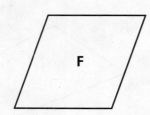
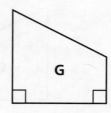
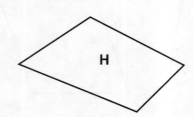

6 Which figures have perpendicular sides?

_____

7 Which figures have exactly one pair of opposite sides parallel?

_____

8 Which figures have two pairs of opposite sides parallel?

_____

9 Which figures have both parallel and perpendicular sides?

_____

10 Which figures have no parallel or perpendicular sides?

_____

✓ **Check Understanding**

Give examples of ways to sort triangles and quadrilaterals.

Classify Polygons

Name _____

Sort Polygons Cards

Cut along the dashed lines.

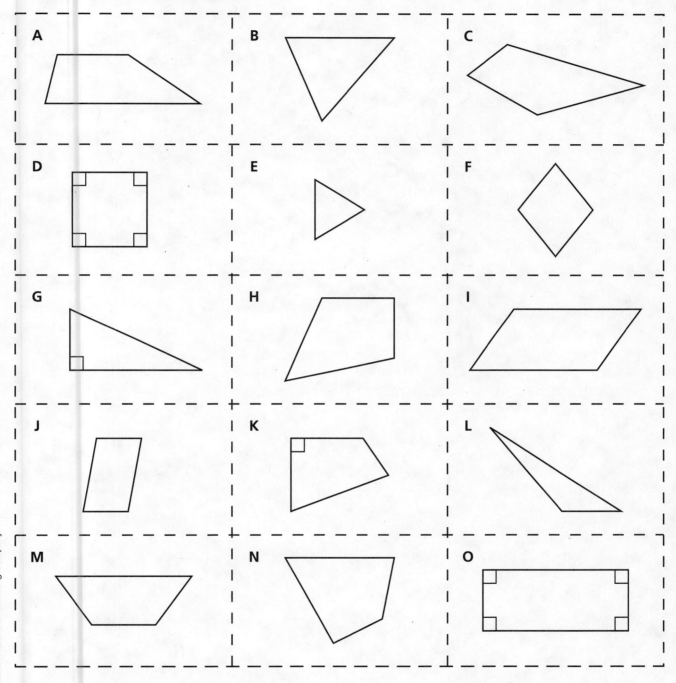

Classify Polygons **396A**

Classify Polygons

Name _____

Identify Line Symmetry in Figures

VOCABULARY
line symmetry
line of symmetry

A plane figure has **line symmetry** if it can be folded along a line so the two halves match exactly. The fold is called a **line of symmetry**.

Does the figure have line symmetry? Write *yes* or *no*.

1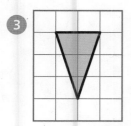

_____

2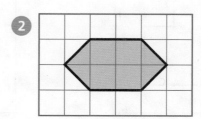

_____

3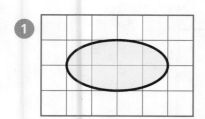

_____

4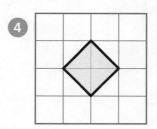

_____

5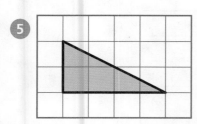

_____

6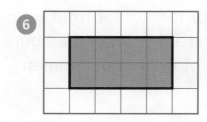

_____

Draw Lines of Symmetry

A line of symmetry divides a figure or design into two matching parts.

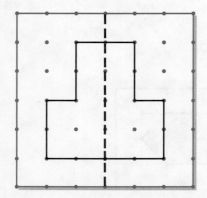 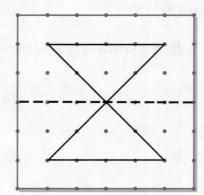

Draw the line of symmetry in the figure or design.

7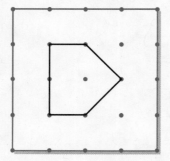

8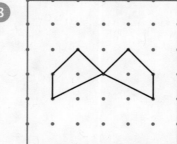

9 Which figures in Exercises 1–6 have more than one line of symmetry?

_____

10 Choose one of the figures from your answer to Exercise 9. Draw the figure and draw all of its lines of symmetry.

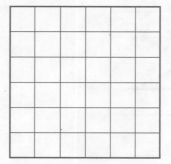

Line Symmetry

What's the Error?

Dear Math Students,

I drew the diagonal of this rectangle as a line of symmetry.

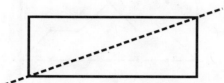

My friend told me I made a mistake. Can you help me figure out what my mistake was?

Your friend,
Puzzled Penguin

11 Write a response to Puzzled Penguin.

_____

_____

_____

_____

_____

_____

_____

_____

_____

_____

Draw the Other Half

Draw the other half of each figure to make a whole figure or design with line symmetry.

12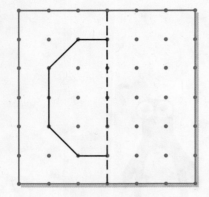

13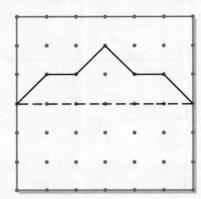

14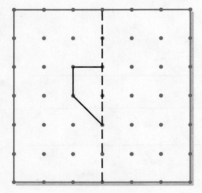

15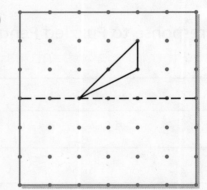

16 Copy one of your answers to Exercises 12–15 onto another piece of paper. Cut out the design and then fold it along the line of symmetry. Check that the two halves of the design match exactly.

 Check Understanding

Which of your completed figures in Exercises 12–15 have more than one line of symmetry? _____

Line Symmetry

Name _____

Math and Flags of the World

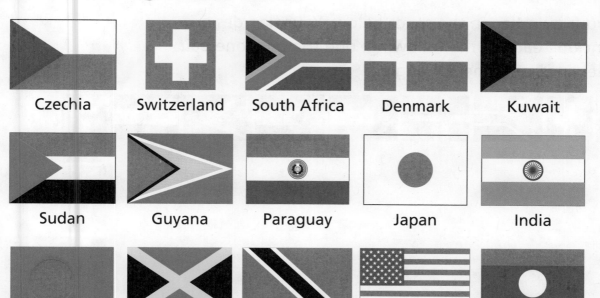

Czechia   Switzerland   South Africa   Denmark   Kuwait

Sudan   Guyana   Paraguay   Japan   India

Bangladesh   Jamaica   Trinidad and Tobago   United States of America   Laos

Flags are used in many different ways. Some sports teams use flags to generate team spirit, a flag might be used to start a race, or a homeowner might use a flag for decoration. States and countries also use flags as a representation of their communities. Each flag is different, both in color and design.

Use the designs on the flags to answer the questions.

1 What types of quadrilaterals are used in the Kuwait flag?

_____

2 How many designs have no parallel lines? Name the flags.

_____

3 How many designs have perpendicular lines? Name the flags.

_____

4 Which designs have at least two lines of symmetry?

_____

Designer Flags

Design your own flag in the space below. Your flag design should include each of the following: one triangle, one pair of parallel lines, and one 30° angle.

5 What type of triangle did you draw in your flag design? Explain how the sides of the triangle helped you classify the triangle.

_____

6 Compare the flag design you made to the flag design that a classmate made. How are the two designs the same? How are they different? What shapes did you use that your classmate did not use?

_____

Focus on Mathematical Practices

Look at the figures.

1 Circle the figure with obtuse angles.

2 Circle the figure that appears to have a right angle.

3 Circle the figure that appears to have perpendicular sides.

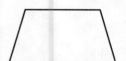  

4 Does the figure have line symmetry?

5 Does the figure have line symmetry?

Name _____ **Date** _____

Add or subtract.

1
```
  352
+ 337
```

2
```
  673
- 460
```

3
```
  6,330
- 4,218
```

4
```
  722
- 518
```

5
```
  387,599
+ 472,850
```

6
```
  81,275
+ 28,952
```

7
```
  5,923
+ 6,057
```

8
```
  8,312
+   974
```

9
```
  529
+ 355
```

10
```
  40,507
- 23,316
```

11
```
  78,342
-  5,761
```

12
```
  34,809
+  7,181
```

13
```
  6,537
- 3,215
```

14
```
  349,744
-  84,589
```

15
```
  800,000
- 526,783
```

1. Draw and label line segment *FG*.

2. Use a protractor to measure the angle.

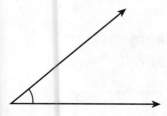

The angle measures _____.

3. Choose the figure that has at least one pair of parallel lines. Mark all that apply.

Ⓐ Ⓑ Ⓒ Ⓓ

4. Use the figures. For 4a–4d, select True or False for the statement.

  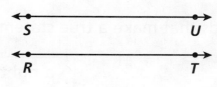

4a. $\overleftrightarrow{ZX}$ and $\overleftrightarrow{WY}$ are parallel.   ○ True   ○ False

4b. $\overleftrightarrow{SU}$ and $\overleftrightarrow{RT}$ are parallel.   ○ True   ○ False

4c. $\overleftrightarrow{ZX}$ and $\overleftrightarrow{WY}$ are perpendicular.   ○ True   ○ False

4d. A line drawn through points *R* and *U* is perpendicular to $\overleftrightarrow{RT}$.   ○ True   ○ False

5 The map below shows a section of Fatima's town.

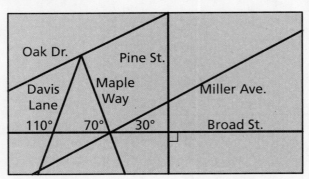

Part A Fatima is walking on Oak Drive and Gabe is walking on Miller Ave. Could Fatima and Gabe ever meet? If so, where?

Part B Which street is perpendicular to Broad St.? Explain how you know.

6 Choose the words that make a true statement.

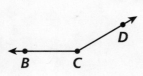

Angle *BCD* is

| a right |
| an acute |
| an obtuse |

angle.

7 Draw all the lines of symmetry for the figure.

8 A gear in a watch has turned clockwise, in one-degree
sections, a total of 300 times.

The gear has turned a total of ☐ degrees.

9 Lucy is designing a block for a quilt. She measured one of the
angles. Use the numbers and symbols on the tiles to write and
solve an equation to find the unknown angle measure.

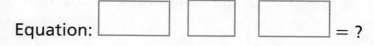

Equation: ☐ ☐ ☐ = ?

Solution: ? = ☐

10 Luke is drawing a figure that has exactly 2 acute angles.
For 10a–10d, choose Yes or No to tell if the figure could be the
figure Luke is drawing.

10a. ◇ ○ Yes ○ No

10b. △ ○ Yes ○ No

10c. ☐ ○ Yes ○ No

10d. ⏢ ○ Yes ○ No

11 Triangle *QRS* can be classified

as | an acute / a right / an obtuse | triangle.

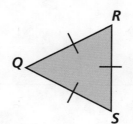

12 Choose the two angles that could be put together to make a 130° angle.

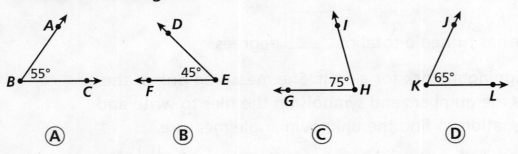

Ⓐ   Ⓑ   Ⓒ   Ⓓ

13 A sign has two pairs of parallel sides and two pairs of equal sides. Name one type of quadrilateral that the sign could be.

14 The circle represents all of the students in a class. Each section represents the students in the class who chose a certain color as their favorite. The angle measures for some sections are given.

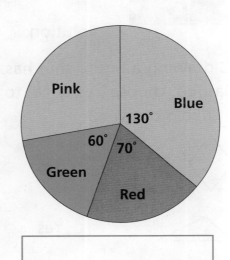

Part A

What is the sum of the angle measures for Blue, Red, and Green?

Part B

Explain how to find the angle measure for Pink. Then find the measure.

15 Draw one diagonal in the figure to form
two obtuse triangles.

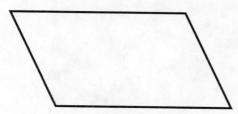

16 Does the figure have a line of symmetry? Explain.

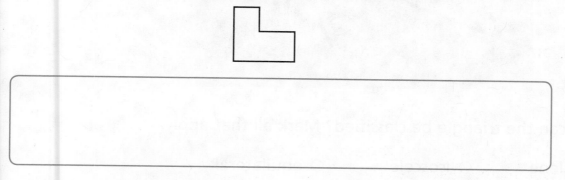

17 A Ferris wheel turns 35° before it pauses.
It turns another 85° before stopping again.

Part A

What is the total measure of the angle
that the Ferris wheel turned?

Part B

How many more times will it need to
repeat the pattern to turn 360°?
Explain your thinking.

18 Cross Street, West Street, and Carmichael Street form a triangle.

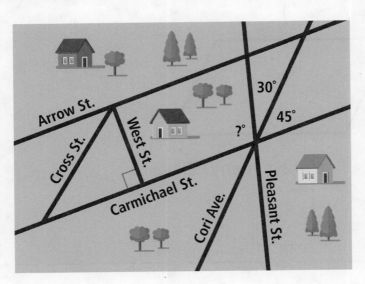

How can the triangle be classified? Mark all that apply.

○ scalene   ○ isosceles   ○ equilateral

○ acute   ○ right   ○ obtuse

19 A stage has four sides with exactly one pair of parallel sides.

Marjorie says the shape of the stage is a quadrilateral and a rectangle. Do you agree? Explain.

20 What is the unknown angle measure in this pattern?

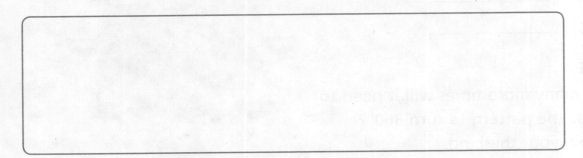

Crack a Secret Code

Meredith developed a secret code using the letters
she labeled these polygons. Use what you know about
polygons to solve each problem.

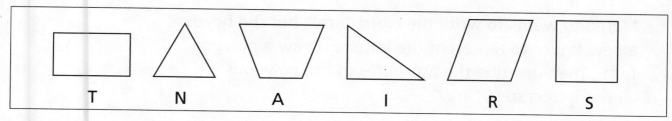

T   N   A   I   R   S

1 Make a word using the letters of all the polygons
that are **not** quadrilaterals.

_____

2 Make a word using the letters of all the polygons
that have parallel sides.

_____

_____

3 Make a word using the letters of all the polygons
that have perpendicular sides.

_____

_____

4 Make a word using the letters of all the polygons
that have acute angles.

_____

_____

5 Meredith wants to use the letters of three polygons
to write the word "ran." Write a description for the
polygons that she can use.

_____

_____

_____

6 Meredith thinks she can use all of the polygons to write "strain" using the description "All polygons that have at least two sides with equal side lengths." Is she correct? If not, which figure or figures do not match the description?

_____

7 Meredith wants to write the word "are," but she needs a new figure to represent the letter E. Draw a polygon for E. Then describe the attributes of the polygons whose letters spell "are."

_____

_____

8 Can you write a description for attributes of polygons whose letters spell the word "ant?" Explain why or why not.

_____

_____

_____

9 Explain how polygons *T* and *R* are alike and different.

_____

_____

_____

_____

10 Write your own description for the polygons whose letters spell a word of your choice. Make sure that the attributes you choose for your description are shared with all of the letters in your word and are not shared with any letters not in your word.

_____

Examples of Metric Units

Length

1 kilometer (km)	1 hectometer (hm)	1 dekameter (dam)	1 meter (m)
about the distance you could walk in 12 minutes 1 km = 1,000 m	about the length of a football field 1 hm = 100 m	about the length of a school bus 1 dam = 10 m	about the distance from the floor to the doorknob

1 decimeter (dm)	1 centimeter (cm)	1 millimeter (mm)
about the length of a new crayon 10 dm = 1 m	about the width of your finger 100 cm = 1 m	about the thickness of a dime 1,000 mm = 1 m

Metric Units

Examples of Metric Units

Liquid Volume

1 kiloliter (kL)	1 liter (L)	1 milliliter (mL)

This cube holds 1 kiloliter of liquid.

$1 \text{ kL} = 1,000 \text{ L}$

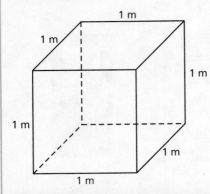

This cube holds 1 liter of liquid.

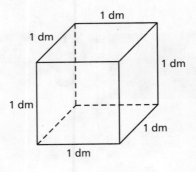

This cube holds 1 milliliter of liquid.

$1,000 \text{ mL} = 1 \text{ L}$

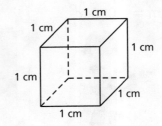

Mass

1 kilogram (kg)	1 gram (g)	1 milligram (mg)

The mass of 5 bananas is about 1 kilogram.

$1 \text{ kg} = 1,000 \text{ g}$

The mass of a paper clip is about 1 gram.

The mass of a pinch of salt is about 1 milligram.

$1,000 \text{ mg} = 1 \text{ g}$

Examples of Customary Units

Length

1 inch (in.)	1 foot (ft)	1 yard (yd)	1 mile (mi)
The distance across a quarter is about 1 inch.	The length of your math book is about 1 foot. 1 ft = 12 in.	The length of a guitar is about 1 yard. 1 yd = 3 ft	You can walk 1 mile in about 20 minutes. 1 mi = 5,280 ft = 1,760 yd

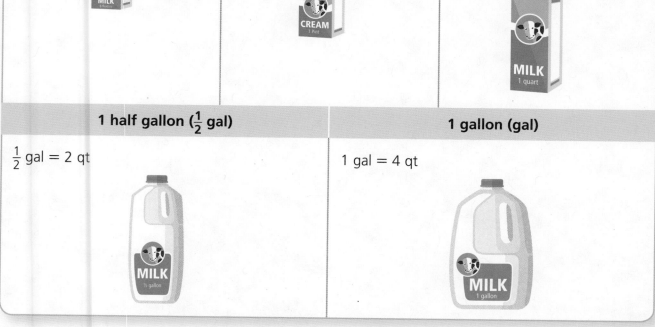

Liquid Volume

1 cup (c)	1 pint (pt)	1 quart (qt)
1 c = 8 fluid ounces	1 pt = 2 c	1 qt = 2 pt = 4 c

1 half gallon ($\frac{1}{2}$ gal)	1 gallon (gal)
$\frac{1}{2}$ gal = 2 qt	1 gal = 4 qt

Customary Units

Examples of Customary Units

Weight

1 ounce (oz)	1 pound (lb)	1 ton (T)
A slice of bread weighs about 1 ounce.	A package of butter weighs 1 pound. 1 lb = 16 oz	A small car weighs about 1 ton. 1 T = 2,000 lb

Table of Measures

Metric	Customary

Length/Area

Metric	Customary
1,000 millimeters (mm) = 1 meter (m)	1 foot (ft) = 12 inches (in.)
100 centimeters (cm) = 1 meter	1 yard (yd) = 36 inches
10 decimeters (dm) = 1 meter	1 yard = 3 feet
1 dekameter (dam) = 10 meters	1 mile (mi) = 5,280 feet
1 hectometer (hm) = 100 meters	1 mile = 1,760 yards
1 kilometer (km) = 1,000 meters	

Liquid Volume

Metric	Customary
1,000 milliliters (mL) = 1 liter (L)	6 teaspoons (tsp) = 1 fluid ounce (fl oz)
100 centiliters (cL) = 1 liter	2 tablespoons (tbsp) = 1 fluid ounce
10 deciliters (dL) = 1 liter	1 cup (c) = 8 fluid ounces
1 dekaliter (daL) = 10 liters	1 pint (pt) = 2 cups
1 hectoliter (hL) = 100 liters	1 quart (qt) = 2 pints
1 kiloliter (kL) = 1,000 liters	1 gallon (gal) = 4 quarts

Mass / Weight

Mass	Weight
1,000 milligrams (mg) = 1 gram (g)	1 pound (lb) = 16 ounces
100 centigrams (cg) = 1 gram	1 ton (T) = 2,000 pounds
10 decigrams (dg) = 1 gram	
1 dekagram (dag) = 10 grams	
1 hectogram (hg) = 100 grams	
1 kilogram (kg) = 1,000 grams	
1 metric ton = 1,000 kilograms	

Reference Tables

Table of Units of Time

Time

1 minute (min) = 60 seconds (sec)	1 year = 365 days
1 hour (hr) = 60 minutes	1 leap year = 366 days
1 day = 24 hours	1 decade = 10 years
1 week (wk) = 7 days	1 century = 100 years
1 month is about 30 days	1 millennium = 1,000 years
1 year (yr) = 12 months (mo) or about 52 weeks	

Table of Formulas

Perimeter

Polygon

P = sum of the lengths of the sides

Rectangle

$P = 2(l + w)$ or $P = 2l + 2w$

Square

$P = 4s$

Area

Rectangle

$A = lw$ or $A = bh$

Square

$A = s \cdot s$

© Houghton Mifflin Harcourt Publishing Company

Properties of Operations

Associative Property of Addition

$(a + b) + c = a + (b + c)$	$(2 + 5) + 3 = 2 + (5 + 3)$

Commutative Property of Addition

$a + b = b + a$	$4 + 6 = 6 + 4$

Addition Identity Property of 0

$a + 0 = 0 + a = a$	$3 + 0 = 0 + 3 = 3$

Associative Property of Multiplication

$(a \cdot b) \cdot c = a \cdot (b \cdot c)$	$(3 \cdot 5) \cdot 7 = 3 \cdot (5 \cdot 7)$

Commutative Property of Multiplication

$a \cdot b = b \cdot a$	$6 \cdot 3 = 3 \cdot 6$

Multiplicative Identity Property of 1

$a \cdot 1 = 1 \cdot a = a$	$8 \cdot 1 = 1 \cdot 8 = 8$

Distributive Property of Multiplication over Addition

$a \cdot (b + c) = (a \cdot b) + (a \cdot c)$	$2 \cdot (4 + 3) = (2 \cdot 4) + (2 \cdot 3)$

Problem Types

Addition and Subtraction Problem Types

	Result Unknown	Change Unknown	Start Unknown
Add to	A glass contained $\frac{3}{4}$ cup of orange juice. Then $\frac{1}{4}$ cup of pineapple juice was added. How much juice is in the glass now? *Situation and solution equation:* [1] $\frac{3}{4} + \frac{1}{4} = c$	A glass contained $\frac{3}{4}$ cup of orange juice. Then some pineapple juice was added. Now the glass contains 1 cup of juice. How much pineapple juice was added? *Situation equation:* $\frac{3}{4} + c = 1$ *Solution equation:* $c = 1 - \frac{3}{4}$	A glass contained some orange juice. Then $\frac{1}{4}$ cup of pineapple juice was added. Now the glass contains 1 cup of juice. How much orange juice was in the glass to start? *Situation equation:* $c + \frac{1}{4} = 1$ *Solution equation:* $c = 1 - \frac{1}{4}$
Take from	Micah had a ribbon $\frac{5}{6}$ yard long. He cut off a piece $\frac{1}{6}$ yard long. What is the length of the ribbon that is left? *Situation and solution equation:* $\frac{5}{6} - \frac{1}{6} = r$	Micah had a ribbon $\frac{5}{6}$ yard long. He cut off a piece. Now the ribbon is $\frac{4}{6}$ yard long. What is the length of the ribbon he cut off? *Situation equation:* $\frac{5}{6} - r = \frac{4}{6}$ *Solution equation:* $r = \frac{5}{6} - \frac{4}{6}$	Micah had a ribbon. He cut off a piece $\frac{1}{6}$ yard long. Now the ribbon is $\frac{4}{6}$ yard long. What was the length of the ribbon he started with? *Situation equation:* $r - \frac{1}{6} = \frac{4}{6}$ *Solution equation:* $r = \frac{4}{6} + \frac{1}{6}$

[1]A situation equation represents the structure (action) in the problem situation. A solution equation shows the operation used to find the answer.

Addition and Subtraction Problem Types (continued)

	Total Unknown	Addend Unknown	Other Addend Unknown
Put Together/ Take Apart	A baker combines $1\frac{2}{3}$ cups of white flour and $\frac{2}{3}$ cup of wheat flour. How much flour is this altogether? *Math drawing:*[1] *Situation and solution equation:* $1\frac{2}{3} + \frac{2}{3} = f$	Of the $2\frac{1}{3}$ cups of flour a baker uses, $1\frac{2}{3}$ cups are white flour. The rest is wheat flour. How much wheat flour does the baker use? *Math drawing:*  *Situation equation:* $2\frac{1}{3} = 1\frac{2}{3} + f$ *Solution equation:* $f = 2\frac{1}{3} - 1\frac{2}{3}$	A baker uses $2\frac{1}{3}$ cups of flour. Some is white flour and $\frac{2}{3}$ cup is wheat flour. How much white flour does the baker use? *Math drawing:* *Situation equation:* $2\frac{1}{3} = f + \frac{2}{3}$ *Solution equation:* $f = 2\frac{1}{3} - \frac{2}{3}$

Both Addends Unknown is a productive extension of this basic situation, especially for finding two fractions with a sum of 1. Such take apart situations can be used to show all the decompositions of a given number. The associated equations, which have the total on the left of the equal sign, help students understand that the = sign does not always mean *makes* or *results in* but always does mean *is the same number as*.

Both Addends Unknown

A baker is making different kinds of bread using only the $\frac{1}{4}$ cup measure. What different mixtures can be made with white flour and wheat flour to total 1 cup?

Math drawing:

Situation equation:
$1 = a + b$

[1]These math drawings are called math mountains in Grades 1–3 and break apart drawings in Grades 4 and 5.

Addition and Subtraction Problem Types (continued)

	Difference Unknown	Greater Unknown	Smaller Unknown
Additive Comparison[1]	At a zoo, the female rhino weighs $1\frac{3}{5}$ tons. The male rhino weighs $2\frac{2}{5}$ tons. How much more does the male rhino weigh than the female rhino?	**Leading Language** At a zoo, the female rhino weighs $1\frac{3}{5}$ tons. The male rhino weighs $\frac{4}{5}$ ton more than the female rhino. How much does the male rhino weigh?	**Leading Language** At a zoo, the male rhino weighs $2\frac{2}{5}$ tons. The female rhino weighs $\frac{4}{5}$ ton less than the male rhino. How much does the female rhino weigh?
	At a zoo, the female rhino weighs $1\frac{3}{5}$ tons. The male rhino weighs $2\frac{2}{5}$ tons. How much less does the female rhino weigh than the male rhino?	**Misleading Language** At a zoo, the female rhino weighs $1\frac{3}{5}$ tons. The female rhino weighs $\frac{4}{5}$ ton less than the male rhino. How much does the male rhino weigh?	**Misleading Language** At a zoo, the male rhino weighs $2\frac{2}{5}$ tons. The male rhino weighs $\frac{4}{5}$ ton more than the female rhino. How much does the female rhino weigh?
	Math drawing:	*Math drawing:*	*Math drawing:*
	$2\frac{2}{5}$ / $1\frac{3}{5}$ d	m / $1\frac{3}{5}$ $\frac{4}{5}$	$2\frac{2}{5}$ / f $\frac{4}{5}$
	Situation equation: $1\frac{3}{5} + d = 2\frac{2}{5}$ or $d = 2\frac{2}{5} - 1\frac{3}{5}$	*Situation and solution equation:* $1\frac{3}{5} + \frac{4}{5} = m$	*Situation equation:* $f + \frac{4}{5} = 2\frac{2}{5}$ or $f = 2\frac{2}{5} - \frac{4}{5}$
	Solution equation: $d = 2\frac{2}{5} - 1\frac{3}{5}$		*Solution equation:* $f = 2\frac{2}{5} - \frac{4}{5}$

[1]A comparison sentence can always be said in two ways. One way uses *more*, and the other uses *fewer* or *less*. Misleading language suggests the wrong operation. For example, it says *the female rhino weighs $\frac{4}{5}$ ton less than the male*, but you have to add $\frac{4}{5}$ ton to the female's weight to get the male's weight.

Multiplication and Division Problem Types

	Product Unknown	Group Size Unknown	Number of Groups Unknown
Equal Groups	A teacher bought 10 boxes of pencils. There are 20 pencils in each box. How many pencils did the teacher buy? *Situation and solution equation:* $p = 10 \cdot 20$	A teacher bought 10 boxes of pencils. She bought 200 pencils in all. How many pencils are in each box? *Situation equation:* $10 \cdot n = 200$ *Solution equation:* $n = 200 \div 10$	A teacher bought boxes of 20 pencils. She bought 200 pencils in all. How many boxes of pencils did she buy *Situation equation:* $b \cdot 20 = 200$ *Solution equation:* $b = 200 \div 20$

	Product Unknown	Factor Unknown	Factor Unknown
Arrays[1]	An auditorium has 60 rows with 30 seats in each row. How many seats are in the auditorium? *Math drawing:* 30 60 | s *Situation and solution equation:* $s = 60 \cdot 30$	An auditorium has 60 rows with the same number of seats in each row. There are 1,800 seats in all. How many seats are in each row? *Math drawing:* n 60 | 1,800 *Situation equation:* $60 \cdot n = 1{,}800$ *Solution equation:* $n = 1{,}800 \div 60$	The 1,800 seats in an auditorium are arranged in rows of 30. How many rows of seats are there? *Math drawing:* 30 r | 1,800 *Situation equation:* $r \cdot 30 = 1{,}800$ *Solution equation:* $r = 1{,}800 \div 30$

[1]We use rectangle models for both array and area problems in Grades 4 and 5 because the numbers in the problems are too large to represent with arrays.

Problem Types

Multiplication and Division Problem Types (continued)

	Product Unknown	Factor Unknown	Factor Unknown
Area	Sophie's backyard is 80 feet long and 40 feet wide. What is the area of Sophie's backyard? Math drawing: 80 40 · A Situation and solution equation: $A = 80 \cdot 40$	Sophie's backyard has an area of 3,200 square feet. The length of the yard is 80 feet. What is the width of the yard? Math drawing: 80 w · 3,200 Situation equation: $80 \cdot w = 3{,}200$ Solution equation: $w = 3{,}200 \div 80$	Sophie's backyard has an area of 3,200 square feet. The width of the yard is 40 feet. What is the length of the yard? Math drawing: l 40 · 3,200 Situation equation: $l \cdot 40 = 3{,}200$ Solution equation: $l = 3{,}200 \div 40$
Multiplicative Comparison	**Multiplier 1: Larger Unknown** Sam has 4 times as many marbles as Brady has. Brady has 70 marbles. How many marbles does Sam have? Math drawing: s	70	70	70	70 | b	70 | $b = s \div 4$ and $s = 4 \cdot b$ Situation and solution equation: $s = 4 \cdot 70$	**Multiplier 1: Smaller Unknown** Sam has 4 times as many marbles as Brady has. Sam has 280 marbles. How many marbles does Brady have? Math drawing: 280 s b $b = s \div 4$ and $s = 4 \cdot b$ Situation equation: $4 \cdot b = 280$ Situation and solution equation: $b = 280 \div 4$	**Multiplier 1: Unknown** Sam has 280 marbles. Brady has 70 marbles. The number of marbles Sam has is how many times the number Brady has? Math drawing: 280 s	70	70	70	70 | b	70 | $m \cdot b = s$ Situation equation: $m \cdot 70 = 280$ Solution equation: $m = 280 \div 70$

© Houghton Mifflin Harcourt Publishing Company

MathWord **Power**

Word Review

Work with a partner. Choose a word from the current unit or a review word from a previous unit. Use the word to complete one of the activities listed on the right. Then ask your partner if they have any edits to your work or questions about what you described. Repeat, having your partner choose a word.

Activities

- Give the meaning in words or gestures.
- Use the word in a sentence.
- Give another word that is related to the word in some way and explain the relationship.

Crossword Puzzle

Create a crossword puzzle similar to the example below. Use vocabulary words from the unit. You can add other related words, too. Challenge your partner to solve the puzzle.

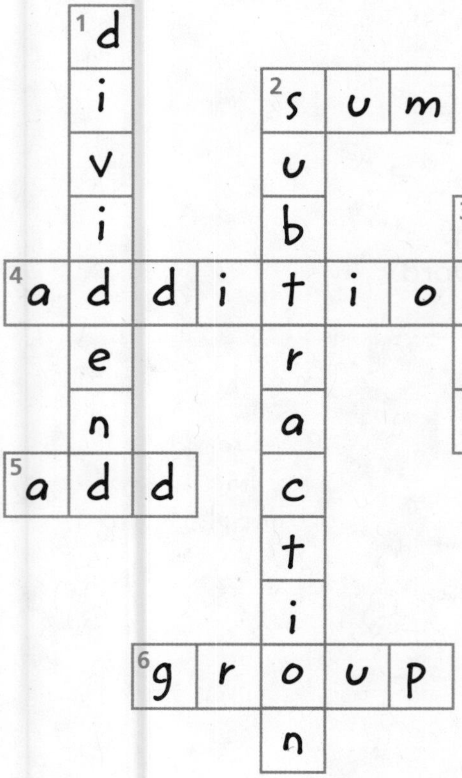

Across

2. The answer to an addition problem
4. _____ and subtraction are inverse operations.
5. To put amounts together
6. When you trade 10 ones for 1 ten, you _____.

Down

1. The number to be divided in a division problem
2. The operation that you can use to find out how much more one number is than another.
3. A fraction with a numerator of 1 is a _____ fraction.

The crossword grid:

- 1 Down: d i v i d e n d
- 2 Across: s u m
- 2 Down: s u b t r a c t i o n
- 3 Down: u n i t
- 4 Across: a d d i t i o n
- 5 Across: a d d
- 6 Across: g r o u p

Vocabulary Activities

Word Wall

With your teacher's permission, start a word wall in your classroom. As you work through each lesson, put the math vocabulary words on index cards and place them on the word wall. You can work with a partner or a small group choosing a word and giving the definition.

Word Web

Make a word web for a word or words you do not understand in a unit. Fill in the web with words or phrases that are related to the vocabulary word.

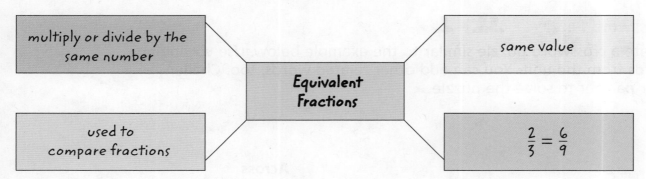

multiply or divide by the same number		same value
	Equivalent Fractions	
used to compare fractions		$\frac{2}{3} = \frac{6}{9}$

Alphabet Challenge

Take an alphabet challenge. Choose 3 letters from the alphabet. Think of three vocabulary words for each letter. Then write the definition or draw an example for each word.

A	E	L
addition Associative Property area	equation expanded form estimate	liter line line plot

Concentration

Write the vocabulary words and related words from a unit on index cards. Write the definitions on a different set of index cards. Choose 3 to 6 pairs of vocabulary words and definitions. Mix up the set of pairs. Then place the cards facedown on a table. Take turns turning over two cards. If one card is a word and one card is a definition that matches the word, take the pair. Continue until each word has been matched with its definition.

area

The number of square units that cover a figure.

Math Journal

As you learn new words, write them in your Math Journal. Write the definition of the word and include a sketch or an example. As you learn new information about the word, add notes to your definition.

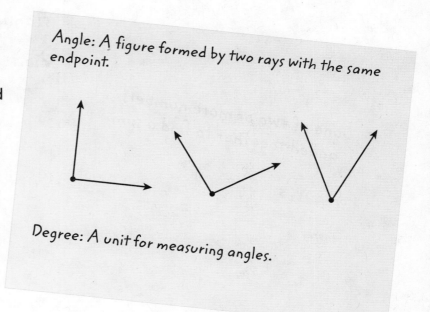

Angle: A figure formed by two rays with the same endpoint.

Degree: A unit for measuring angles.

Vocabulary Activities

What's the Word?

Work together to make a poster or bulletin board display of the words in a unit. Write definitions on a set of index cards. Mix up the cards. Work with a partner, choosing a definition from the index cards. Have your partner point to the word on the poster and name the matching math vocabulary word. Switch roles and try the activity again.

array

place value

addend

inverse operations

expanded form

word form

standard form

digit

one of two or more numbers added together to find a sum

A

acute angle
An angle smaller than a right angle.

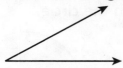

acute triangle
A triangle with three acute angles.

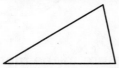

addend
One of two or more numbers added together to find a sum.

Example:

$$7 + 8 = 15$$

addend   addend   sum

adjacent sides
Two sides that meet at a point.

Example:
Sides *a* and *b* are adjacent.

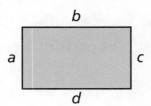

Algebraic Notation Method*
A strategy based on the Distributive Property in which a factor is decomposed to create simpler algebraic expressions, and the Distributive Property is applied.

Example:

$9 \cdot 28 = 9 \cdot (20 + 8)$

$\quad\quad = (9 \cdot 20) + (9 \cdot 8)$

$\quad\quad = 180 + 72$

$\quad\quad = 252$

analog clock
A clock with a face and hands.

angle
A figure formed by two rays with the same endpoint.

area
The number of square units that cover a figure.

array
An arrangement of objects, symbols, or numbers in rows and columns.

Associative Property of Addition
Grouping the addends in different ways does not change the sum.

Example:

$3 + (5 + 7) = 15$

$(3 + 5) + 7 = 15$

*A classroom research-based term developed for *Math Expressions*

Glossary

Associative Property of Multiplication
Grouping the factors in different ways does not change the product.

Example:
$3 \times (5 \times 7) = 105$
$(3 \times 5) \times 7 = 105$

B

bar graph
A graph that uses bars to show data. The bars may be vertical or horizontal.

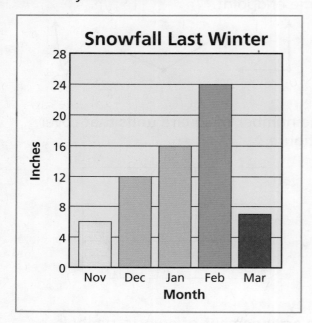

break-apart drawing*
A diagram that shows two addends and the sum.

C

center
The point that is the same distance from every point on the circle.

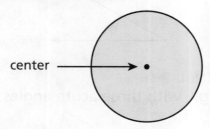

centimeter (cm)
A unit of measure in the metric system that equals one hundredth of a meter.
100 cm = 1 m

circle
A plane figure that forms a closed path so that all the points on the path are the same distance from a point called the center.

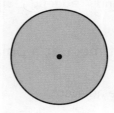

circle graph
A graph that uses parts of a circle to show data.

Example:

*A classroom research-based term developed for *Math Expressions*

© Houghton Mifflin Harcourt Publishing Company

column
A part of a table or array that contains items arranged vertically.

$$\begin{matrix} \bullet & \bullet & \bullet & \bullet \\ \bullet & \bullet & \bullet & \bullet \\ \bullet & \bullet & \bullet & \bullet \\ \bullet & \bullet & \bullet & \bullet \end{matrix}$$

common denominator
A common multiple of two or more denominators.

Example:
A common denominator of $\frac{1}{2}$ and $\frac{1}{3}$ is 6 because 6 is a multiple of 2 and 3.

Commutative Property of Addition
Changing the order of addends does not change the sum.

Example: $3 + 8 = 11$
$8 + 3 = 11$

Commutative Property of Multiplication
Changing the order of factors does not change the product.

Example: $3 \times 8 = 24$
$8 \times 3 = 24$

compare
Describe quantities as greater than, less than, or equal to each other.

comparison bars*
Bars that represent the larger amount and smaller amount in a comparison situation.

For addition and subtraction:

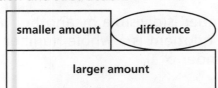

For multiplication and division:

smaller amount	smaller amount	smaller amount	larger amount

smaller amount		

comparison situation*
A situation in which two amounts are compared by addition or by multiplication. An *addition comparison situation* compares by asking or telling how much more (how much less) one amount is than another. A *multiplication comparison situation* compares by asking or telling how many times as many one amount is as another. The multiplication comparison may also be made using fraction language. For example, you can say, "Sally has one fourth as much as Tom has," instead of saying "Tom has 4 times as much as Sally has."

composite number
A number greater than 1 that has more than one factor pair. Examples of composite numbers are 10 and 18. The factor pairs of 10 are 1 and 10, 2 and 5. The factor pairs of 18 are 1 and 18, 2 and 9, 3 and 6.

cup (c)
A unit of liquid volume in the customary system that equals 8 fluid ounces.

D

data
A collection of information.

decimal number
A representation of a number using the numerals 0 to 9, in which each digit has a value 10 times the digit to its right. A dot or **decimal point** separates the whole-number part of the number on the left from the fractional part on the right.

Examples:
1.23 and 0.3

*A classroom research-based term developed for *Math Expressions*

Glossary

decimal point
A symbol used to separate dollars and cents in money amounts or to separate ones and tenths in decimal numbers.

Examples:

$8.59   1.2

↑   ↑

decimal point

decimeter (dm)
A unit of measure in the metric system that equals one tenth of a meter.
10 dm = 1 m

degree (°)
A unit for measuring angles.

denominator
The number below the bar in a fraction. It shows the total number of equal parts in the whole.

Example:

$\frac{3}{4}$ ←— denominator

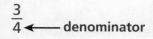

diagonal of a quadrilateral
A line segment that connects two opposite corners (vertices).

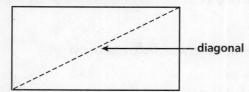

— diagonal

difference
The result of a subtraction.

Example:
54 − 37 = 17 ← difference

digit
Any of the symbols 0, 1, 2, 3, 4, 5, 6, 7, 8, or 9.

digital clock
A clock that shows us the hour and minutes with numbers.

AM 9:30

Digit-by-Digit*
A method used to solve a division problem.

Put in only one digit at a time.

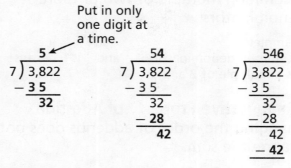

$$
\begin{array}{r}
5 \\
7\overline{)3{,}822} \\
-35 \\
\hline
32
\end{array}
\qquad
\begin{array}{r}
54 \\
7\overline{)3{,}822} \\
-35 \\
\hline
32 \\
-28 \\
\hline
42
\end{array}
\qquad
\begin{array}{r}
546 \\
7\overline{)3{,}822} \\
-35 \\
\hline
32 \\
-28 \\
\hline
42 \\
-42
\end{array}
$$

Distributive Property
You can multiply a sum by a number, or multiply each addend by the number and add the products; the result is the same.

Example:
3 × (2 + 4) = (3 × 2) + (3 × 4)
3 × 6   =   6 + 12
18   =   18

dividend
The number that is divided in division.

Example:

$$
\begin{array}{r}
7 \\
9\overline{)63}
\end{array}
$$

63 is the dividend.

divisible
A number is divisible by another number if the quotient is a whole number with a remainder of 0.

divisor
The number you divide by in division.

Example:

$$
\begin{array}{r}
7 \\
9\overline{)63}
\end{array}
$$

9 is the divisor.

*A classroom research-based term developed for *Math Expressions*

dot array

An arrangement of dots in rows and columns.

E

elapsed time

The time that passes between the beginning and the end of an activity.

endpoint

The point at either end of a line segment or the beginning point of a ray.

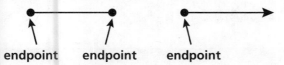

endpoint   endpoint   endpoint

equation

A statement that two expressions are equal. It has an equal sign.

Examples:
$32 + 35 = 67$
$67 = 32 + 34 + 1$
$(7 \times 8) + 1 = 57$

equilateral triangle

Having all sides of equal length.

equivalent fractions

Two or more fractions that represent the same number.

Example:
$\frac{2}{4}$ and $\frac{4}{8}$ are equivalent because they both represent one half.

estimate

A number close to an exact amount or to find about how many or how much.

evaluate an expression

Substitute a value for a letter (or symbol) and then simplify the expression.

expanded form

A way of writing a number that shows the value of each of its digits.

Example:
Expanded form of 835:
$800 + 30 + 5$
8 hundreds + 3 tens + 5 ones

Expanded Notation Method*

A method used to solve multiplication and division problems.

Examples:

$$43 \times 67$$

$$
\begin{array}{r}
67 = 60 + 7 \\
\times\, 43 = 40 + 3 \\
\hline
40 \times 60 = 2400 \\
40 \times 7 \ = \ 280 \\
3 \times 60 \ = \ 180 \\
3 \times 7 \ \ = + 21 \\
\hline
2{,}881
\end{array}
$$

$$3{,}822 \div 7$$

$$
\begin{array}{r}
6 \\
40 \,\big)\, 546 \\
500 \\
7\,\overline{)\,3{,}822} \\
-\,3\,500 \\
\hline
322 \\
-\,280 \\
\hline
42 \\
-\,42 \\
\hline
0
\end{array}
$$

*A classroom research-based term developed for *Math Expressions*

expression

A number, variable, or a combination of numbers and variables with one or more operations.

Examples:

4

$6x$

$6x - 5$

$7 + 4$

F

factor

One of two or more numbers multiplied to find a product.

Example:

$$4 \times 5 = 20$$

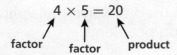

factor · factor · product

factor pair

A factor pair for a number is a pair of whole numbers whose product is that number.

Example:

$$5 \times 7 = 35$$

factor pair · product

fluid ounce (fl oz)

A unit of liquid volume in the customary system.

8 fluid ounces = 1 cup

foot (ft)

A U.S. customary unit of length equal to 12 inches.

formula

An equation with letters or symbols that describes a rule.

The formula for the area of a rectangle is:

$$A = l \times w$$

where A is the area, l is the length, and w is the width.

fraction

A number that is the sum of unit fractions, each an equal part of a set or part of a whole.

Examples:

$$\frac{3}{4} = \frac{1}{4} + \frac{1}{4} + \frac{1}{4}$$

$$\frac{5}{4} = \frac{1}{4} + \frac{1}{4} + \frac{1}{4} + \frac{1}{4} + \frac{1}{4}$$

G

gallon (gal)

A unit of liquid volume in the customary system that equals 4 quarts.

gram (g)

The basic unit of mass in the metric system.

greater than (>)

A symbol used to compare two numbers. The greater number is given first below.

Example:

33 > 17

33 is greater than 17.

group

To combine numbers to form new tens, hundreds, thousands, and so on.

H

hundredth
A unit fraction representing one of one hundred parts, written as 0.01 or $\frac{1}{100}$.

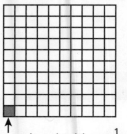

7.634
↑
hundredth

one hundredth = $\frac{1}{100}$ = 0.01

I

Identity Property of Multiplication
The product of 1 and any number equals that number.

Example:
$10 \times 1 = 10$

inch
A U.S. customary unit of length.

Example:

|——— 1 inch ———|

inequality
A statement that two expressions are not equal.

Examples:
$2 < 5$
$4 + 5 > 12 - 8$

inverse operations
Opposite or reverse operations that undo each other. Addition and subtraction are inverse operations. Multiplication and division are inverse operations.

Examples:
$4 + 6 = 10$ so, $10 - 6 = 4$ and $10 - 4 = 6$.
$3 \times 9 = 27$ so, $27 \div 9 = 3$ and $27 \div 3 = 9$.

isosceles triangle
A triangle with at least two sides of equal length.

K

kilogram (kg)
A unit of mass in the metric system that equals one thousand grams.

1 kg = 1,000 g

kiloliter (kL)
A unit of liquid volume in the metric system that equals one thousand liters.

1 kL = 1,000 L

kilometer (km)
A unit of length in the metric system that equals 1,000 meters.

1 km = 1,000 m

L

least common denominator
The least common multiple of two or more denominators.

Example:
The least common denominator of $\frac{1}{2}$ and $\frac{1}{3}$ is 6 because 6 is the smallest multiple of 2 and 3.

length
The measure of a line segment or the distance across the longer side of a rectangle

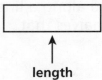

length

Glossary

less than (<)
A symbol used to compare two numbers. The smaller number is given first below.

Example:
54 < 78
54 is less than 78.

line
A straight path that goes on forever in opposite directions.

Example:
line *AB*

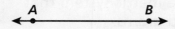

line of symmetry
A line on which a figure can be folded so that the two halves match exactly.

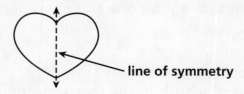

line of symmetry

line plot
A diagram that shows the frequency of data on a number line. Also called a dot plot.

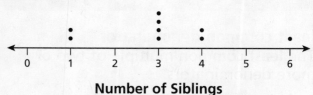

Number of Siblings

line segment
Part of a line that has two endpoints.

line symmetry
A figure has line symmetry if it can be folded along a line to create two halves that match exactly.

liquid volume
A measure of the space a liquid occupies.

liter (L)
The basic unit of liquid volume in the metric system.
1 liter = 1,000 milliliters

M

mass
The measure of the amount of matter in an object.

meter (m)
The basic unit of length in the metric system.

metric system
A base ten system of measurement.

mile (mi)
A U.S. customary unit of length equal to 5,280 feet.

milligram (mg)
A unit of mass in the metric system.
1,000 mg = 1g

milliliter (mL)
A unit of liquid volume in the metric system. 1,000 mL = 1 L

millimeter (mm)
A unit of length in the metric system.
1,000 mm = 1 m

mixed number
A number that can be represented by a whole number and a fraction.

Example:
$4\frac{1}{2} = 4 + \frac{1}{2}$

multiple

A number that is the product of a given number and any whole number.

Examples:

$4 \times 1 = 4$, so 4 is a multiple of 4.

$4 \times 2 = 8$, so 8 is a multiple of 4.

N

number line

A line that extends, without end, in each direction and shows numbers as a series of points. The location of each number is shown by its distance from 0.

numerator

The number above the bar in a fraction. It shows the number of equal parts.

Example:

$\frac{3}{4}$ ←— numerator $\frac{3}{4} = \frac{1}{4} + \frac{1}{4} + \frac{1}{4}$

O

obtuse angle

An angle greater than a right angle and less than a straight angle.

obtuse triangle

A triangle with one obtuse angle.

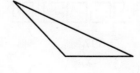

opposite sides

Sides that are across from each other; they do not meet at a point.

Example:

Sides a and c are opposite.

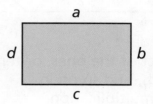

Order of Operations

A set of rules that state the order in which operations should be done.

STEP 1: Compute inside parentheses first.

STEP 2: Multiply and divide from left to right.

STEP 3: Add and subtract from left to right.

ounce (oz)

A unit of weight.

16 ounces = 1 pound

A unit of liquid volume (also called a fluid ounce).

8 ounces = 1 cup

P

parallel lines

Lines in the same plane that never intersect are parallel. Line segments and rays that are part of parallel lines are also parallel.

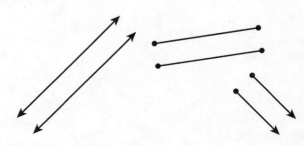

Glossary

parallelogram

A quadrilateral with both pairs of opposite sides parallel.

partial product

The product of the ones, or tens, or hundreds, and so on in multidigit multiplication.

Example:

```
    24
  ×  9
    36   ←  partial product (9 × 4)
   180   ←  partial product (9 × 20)
   216
```

pattern

A sequence that can be described by a rule.

perimeter

The distance around a figure.

perpendicular lines

Lines, line segments, or rays are perpendicular if they form right angles.

Example:
These two lines are perpendicular.

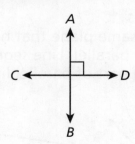

pictograph

A graph that uses pictures or symbols to represent data.

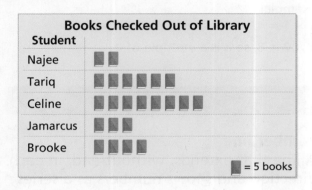

pint (pt)

A customary unit of liquid volume that equals 16 fluid ounces.

place value

The value assigned to the place that a digit occupies in a number.

Example:
235

The 2 is in the hundreds place, so its value is 200.

place value drawing*

A drawing that represents a number. Thousands are represented by vertical rectangles, hundreds are represented by squares, tens are represented by vertical lines, and ones by small circles.

Example:

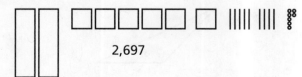

2,697

*A classroom research-based term developed for *Math Expressions*

Place Value Sections Method*
A method using rectangle drawings to solve multiplication or division problems.

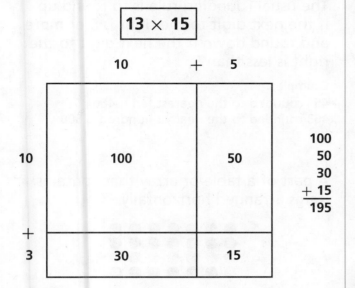

13 × 15

	10	+	5
10	100		50
+			
3	30		15

100
50
30
+ 15
195

330 ÷ 5

a.

5	330

b.

	60
5	330
	− 300
	30

c.

	60 +
5	330
	− 300
	30

d.

	60 +	
5	330	30
	− 300	
	30	

e.

	60 +	6
5	330	30
	− 300	− 30
	30	

f.

	60 +	6 = 66
5	330	30
	− 300	− 30
	30	0

point
A location in a plane. It is usually shown by a dot.

polygon
A closed plane figure with sides made of straight line segments.

pound (lb)
A unit of weight in the U.S. customary system.

prefix
A letter or group of letters placed before a word to make a new word.

prime number
A number greater than 1 that has 1 and itself as the only factor pair. Examples of prime numbers are 2, 7, and 13. The only factor pair of 7 is 1 and 7.

product
The answer to a multiplication problem.

Example:
$9 \times 7 = 63$

product

protractor
A semicircular tool for measuring and constructing angles.

Q

quadrilateral
A polygon with four sides.

quart (qt)
A customary unit of liquid volume that equals 32 ounces or 4 cups.

quotient
The answer to a division problem.

Example:

$$9\overline{)63}^{\,7}$$

7 is the quotient.

R

ray
Part of a line that has one endpoint and extends without end in one direction.

*A classroom research-based term developed for *Math Expressions*

Glossary

rectangle

A parallelogram with four right angles.

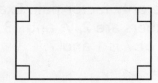

reflex angle

An angle with a measure that is greater than 180° and less than 360°.

remainder

The number left over after dividing two numbers that are not evenly divisible.

Example:

$$5\overline{)43} \quad \begin{array}{c}8\text{ R3}\end{array}$$ The remainder is 3.

rhombus

A parallelogram with sides of equal length.

right angle

One of four angles made by perpendicular line segments.

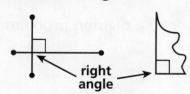

right angle

right triangle

A triangle with one right angle.

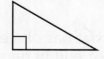

rounding

Finding the nearest ten, hundred, thousand, or some other place value. The usual rounding rule is to round up if the next digit to the right is 5 or more and round down if the next digit to the right is less than 5.

Examples:
463 rounded to the nearest ten is 460.
463 rounded to the nearest hundred is 500.

row

A part of a table or array that contains items arranged horizontally.

S

scalene triangle

A triangle with no equal sides is a scalene triangle.

Shortcut Method*

A strategy for multiplying. It is the current common method in the United States.

Step 1	Step 2
$\begin{array}{r}\overset{7}{28}\\ \times\ 9\\ \hline 2\end{array}$	$\begin{array}{r}\overset{7}{28}\\ \times\ 9\\ \hline 252\end{array}$

*A classroom research-based term developed for *Math Expressions*

simplest form

A fraction is in simplest form if there is no whole number (other than 1) that divides evenly into the numerator and denominator.

Example:

$\frac{3}{4}$ This fraction is in simplest form because no number divides evenly into 3 and 4.

simplify an expression

Combining like terms and performing operations until all possible terms have been combined.

simplify a fraction

Dividing the numerator and the denominator of a fraction by the same number to make an equivalent fraction made from fewer but larger unit fractions.

Example:

$$\frac{5}{10} = \frac{5 \div 5}{10 \div 5} = \frac{1}{2}$$

situation equation*

An equation that shows the structure of the information in a problem.

Example:

$35 + n = 40$

solution equation*

An equation that shows the operation that can be used to solve the problem.

Example:

$n = 40 - 35$

square

A rectangle with 4 sides of equal length and 4 right angles. It is also a rhombus.

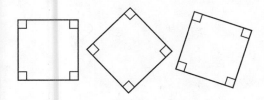

square array

An array in which the number of rows equals the number of columns.

square centimeter (cm²)

A unit of area equal to the area of a square with one-centimeter sides.

square decimeter (dm²)

A unit of area equal to the area of a square with one-decimeter sides.

square foot (ft²)

A unit of area equal to the area of a square with one-foot sides.

square inch (in.²)

A unit of area equal to the area of a square with one-inch sides.

square kilometer (km²)

A unit of area equal to the area of a square with one-kilometer sides.

square meter (m²)

A unit of area equal to the area of a square with one-meter sides.

square mile (mi²)

A unit of area equal to the area of a square with one-mile sides.

square millimeter (mm²)

A unit of area equal to the area of a square with one-millimeter sides.

*A classroom research-based term developed for *Math Expressions*

square unit (unit²)
A unit of area equal to the area of a square with one-unit sides.

square yard (yd²)
A unit of area equal to the area of a square with one-yard sides.

standard form
The form of a number written using digits.

Example:
2,145

straight angle
An angle that measures 180°.

sum
The answer when adding two or more addends.

Example:

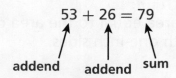

$$53 + 26 = 79$$

addend · addend · sum

T

table
Data arranged in rows and columns.

tenth
A unit fraction representing one of ten equal parts of a whole, written as 0.1 or $\frac{1}{10}$.

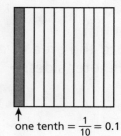

12.34

tenth

one tenth $= \frac{1}{10} = 0.1$

---

term
A number, variable, product, or quotient in an expression or equation. Each term is separated by an operation sign (+, −).

Example:
$3n + 5$ has two terms, $3n$ and 5.

thousandth
A unit fraction representing one of one thousand equal parts of a whole, written as 0.001 or $\frac{1}{1,000}$.

ton
A unit of weight that equals 2,000 pounds.

tonne
A metric unit of mass that equals 1,000 kilograms.

total
Sum. The result of addition.

Example:

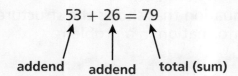

$$53 + 26 = 79$$

addend · addend · total (sum)

trapezoid
A quadrilateral with exactly one pair of parallel sides.

triangle
A polygon with three sides.

U

unit
A standard of measurement.

Examples:
Centimeters, pounds, inches, and so on.

unit fraction
A fraction whose numerator is 1. It shows one equal part of a whole.

Example:

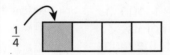

V

variable
A letter or a symbol that represents a number in an algebraic expression.

vertex of an angle
A point that is shared by two sides of an angle.

vertex

vertex of a polygon
A point that is shared by two sides of a polygon.

vertex

W

width
The distance across the shorter side of a rectangle.

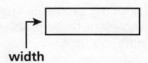

width

word form
The form of a number written using words instead of digits.

Example:
Six hundred thirty-nine

Y

yard (yd)
A U.S. customary unit of length equal to 3 feet.

Common Core State Standards for Mathematical Content

4.OA Operations and Algebraic Thinking	
Use the four operations with whole numbers to solve problems.	
4.OA.A.1	Interpret a multiplication equation as a comparison, e.g., interpret $35 = 5 \times 7$ as a statement that 35 is 5 times as many as 7 and 7 times as many as 5. Represent verbal statements of multiplicative comparisons as multiplication equations.	Unit 4 Lessons 4, 5, 6, 12
4.OA.A.2	Multiply or divide to solve word problems involving multiplicative comparison, e.g., by using drawings and equations with a symbol for the unknown number to represent the problem, distinguishing multiplicative comparison from additive comparison.	Unit 4 Lessons 4, 5, 6, 12
4.OA.A.3	Solve multistep word problems posed with whole numbers and having whole-number answers using the four operations, including problems in which remainders must be interpreted. Represent these problems using equations with a letter standing for the unknown quantity. Assess the reasonableness of answers using mental computation and estimation strategies including rounding.	Unit 1 Lessons 8, 11, 12 Unit 2 Lessons 11, 15, 17, 18, 19 Unit 3 Lessons 8, 9, 10, 11 Unit 4 Lessons 7, 8, 9, 12
Gain familiarity with factors and multiples.	
4.OA.B.4	Find all factor pairs for a whole number in the range 1–100. Recognize that a whole number is a multiple of each of its factors. Determine whether a given whole number in the range 1–100 is a multiple of a given one-digit number. Determine whether a given whole number in the range 1–100 is prime or composite.	Unit 4 Lessons 10, 12
Generate and analyze patterns.	
4.OA.C.5	Generate a number or shape pattern that follows a given rule. Identify apparent features of the pattern that were not explicit in the rule itself.	Unit 4 Lessons 10, 11, 12 Unit 8 Lesson 12

■ Major ■ Supporting ■ Additional

© Houghton Mifflin Harcourt Publishing Company

Common Core State Standards for Mathematical Content

4.NBT Number and Operations in Base Ten

Generalize place value understanding for multi-digit whole numbers.

4.NBT.A.1	Recognize that in a multi-digit whole number, a digit in one place represents ten times what it represents in the place to its right.	Unit 1 Lessons 1, 2, 4 Unit 2 Lessons 2, 3
4.NBT.A.2	Read and write multi-digit whole numbers using base-ten numerals, number names, and expanded form. Compare two multi-digit numbers based on meanings of the digits in each place, using >, =, and < symbols to record the results of comparisons.	Unit 1 Lessons 2, 3, 4, 5 Unit 2 Lessons 4, 10, 12, 16, 19
4.NBT.A.3	Use place value understanding to round multi-digit whole numbers to any place.	Unit 1 Lessons 3, 5, 8, 11, 14 Unit 2 Lessons 5, 17 Unit 3 Lesson 8

Use place value understanding and properties of operations to perform multi-digit arithmetic.

4.NBT.B.4	Fluently add and subtract multi-digit whole numbers using the standard algorithm.	Unit 1 Lessons 6, 7, 8, 9, 10, 11, 12, 13, 14 Unit 4 Lessons 1, 2, 12
4.NBT.B.5	Multiply a whole number of up to four digits by a one-digit whole number, and multiply two two-digit numbers, using strategies based on place value and the properties of operations. Illustrate and explain the calculation by using equations, rectangular arrays, and/or area models.	Unit 2 Lessons 1, 2, 3, 4, 5, 6, 7, 8, 9, 10, 11, 12, 13, 14, 15, 16, 17, 18, 19 Unit 4 Lessons 1, 3, 12
4.NBT.B.6	Find whole-number quotients and remainders with up to four-digit dividends and one-digit divisors, using strategies based on place value, the properties of operations, and/or the relationship between multiplication and division. Illustrate and explain the calculation by using equations, rectangular arrays, and/or area models.	Unit 3 Lessons 1, 2, 3, 4, 5, 6, 7, 8, 9, 10, 11 Unit 4 Lessons 1, 3, 4, 12

4.NF Number and Operations—Fractions

Extend understanding of fraction equivalence and ordering.

4.NF.A.1	Explain why a fraction $\frac{a}{b}$ is equivalent to a fraction $\frac{(n \times a)}{(n \times b)}$ by using visual fraction models, with attention to how the number and size of the parts differ even though the two fractions themselves are the same size. Use this principle to recognize and generate equivalent fractions.	Unit 7 Lessons 4, 5, 6, 13
4.NF.A.2	Compare two fractions with different numerators and different denominators, e.g., by creating common denominators or numerators, or by comparing to a benchmark fraction such as $\frac{1}{2}$. Recognize that comparisons are valid only when the two fractions refer to the same whole. Record the results of comparisons with symbols >, =, or <, and justify the conclusions, e.g., by using a visual fraction model.	Unit 6 Lessons 2, 4, 5, 10 Unit 7 Lessons 1, 2, 3, 6, 13

Build fractions from unit fractions by applying and extending previous understandings of operations on whole numbers.

4.NF.B.3	Understand a fraction $\frac{a}{b}$ with $a > 1$ as a sum of fractions $\frac{1}{b}$.	Unit 6 Lessons 1, 2, 3, 4, 5, 6
4.NF.B.3.a	Understand addition and subtraction of fractions as joining and separating parts referring to the same whole.	Unit 6 Lessons 2, 3, 4, 5, 6, 10
4.NF.B.3.b	Decompose a fraction into a sum of fractions with the same denominator in more than one way, recording each decomposition by an equation. Justify decompositions, e.g., by using a visual fraction model.	Unit 6 Lessons 2, 4, 6
4.NF.B.3.c	Add and subtract mixed numbers with like denominators, e.g., by replacing each mixed number with an equivalent fraction, and/or by using properties of operations and the relationship between addition and subtraction.	Unit 6 Lessons 5, 6, 9, 10
4.NF.B.3.d	Solve word problems involving addition and subtraction of fractions referring to the same whole and having like denominators, e.g., by using visual fraction models and equations to represent the problem.	Unit 6 Lessons 3, 4, 6, 9, 10
4.NF.B.4	Apply and extend previous understandings of multiplication to multiply a fraction by a whole number.	Unit 6 Lessons 7, 8, 9
4.NF.B.4.a	Understand a fraction $\frac{a}{b}$ as a multiple of $\frac{1}{b}$.	Unit 6 Lessons 1, 7, 8, 9
4.NF.B.4.b	Understand a multiple of $\frac{a}{b}$ as a multiple of $\frac{1}{b}$, and use this understanding to multiply a fraction by a whole number.	Unit 6 Lessons 7, 8, 9
4.NF.B.4.c	Solve word problems involving multiplication of a fraction by a whole number, e.g., by using visual fraction models and equations to represent the problem.	Unit 6 Lessons 7, 8, 9, 10

■ **Major**   ■ **Supporting**   ■ **Additional**

Understand decimal notation for fractions, and compare decimal fractions. ■

4.NF.C.5	Express a fraction with denominator 10 as an equivalent fraction with denominator 100, and use this technique to add two fractions with respective denominators 10 and 100.	Unit 7 Lesson 6
4.NF.C.6	Use decimal notation for fractions with denominators 10 or 100.	Unit 7 Lessons 8, 9, 10, 11, 13
4.NF.C.7	Compare two decimals to hundredths by reasoning about their size. Recognize that comparisons are valid only when the two decimals refer to the same whole. Record the results of comparisons with the symbols >, =, or <, and justify the conclusions, e.g., by using a visual model.	Unit 7 Lessons 10, 12, 13

4.MD Measurement and Data

Solve problems involving measurement and conversion of measurements from a larger unit to a smaller unit. ■

4.MD.A.1	Know relative sizes of measurement units within one system of units including km, m, cm; kg, g; lb, oz.; l, ml; hr, min, sec. Within a single system of measurement, express measurements in a larger unit in terms of a smaller unit. Record measurement equivalents in a two-column table.	Unit 5 Lessons 1, 2, 3, 4, 5, 7, 8
4.MD.A.2	Use the four operations to solve word problems involving distances, intervals of time, liquid volumes, masses of objects, and money, including problems involving simple fractions or decimals, and problems that require expressing measurements given in a larger unit in terms of a smaller unit. Represent measurement quantities using diagrams such as number line diagrams that feature a measurement scale.	Unit 1 Lessons 6, 13, 14 Unit 2 Lessons 4, 6, 10, 11, 18, 19 Unit 3 Lesson 8 Unit 4 Lessons 7, 8, 12 Unit 5 Lessons 1, 2, 3, 4, 5, 7, 8 Unit 6 Lessons 3, 6, 7, 8, 9, 10 Unit 7 Lessons 10, 12
4.MD.A.3	Apply the area and perimeter formulas for rectangles in real world and mathematical problems.	Unit 5 Lessons 6, 7, 8

Represent and interpret data. ■

4.MD.B.4	Make a line plot to display a data set of measurements in fractions of a unit ($\frac{1}{2}$, $\frac{1}{4}$, $\frac{1}{8}$). Solve problems involving addition and subtraction of fractions by using information presented in line plots.	Unit 5 Lesson 3 Unit 6 Lesson 6 Unit 7 Lessons 7, 13

Geometric measurement: understand concepts of angle and measure angles.

4.MD.C.5	Recognize angles as geometric shapes that are formed wherever two rays share a common endpoint, and understand concepts of angle measurement:	Unit 8 Lessons 1, 2, 3
4.MD.C.5.a	An angle is measured with reference to a circle with its center at the common endpoint of the rays, by considering the fraction of the circular arc between the points where the two rays intersect the circle. An angle that turns through $\frac{1}{360}$ of a circle is called a "one-degree angle," and can be used to measure angles.	Unit 8 Lessons 2, 3
4.MD.C.5.b	An angle that turns through n one-degree angles is said to have an angle measure of n degrees.	Unit 8 Lessons 2, 3
4.MD.C.6	Measure angles in whole-number degrees using a protractor. Sketch angles of specified measure.	Unit 8 Lessons 2, 3, 5
4.MD.C.7	Recognize angle measure as additive. When an angle is decomposed into non-overlapping parts, the angle measure of the whole is the sum of the angle measures of the parts. Solve addition and subtraction problems to find unknown angles on a diagram in real world and mathematical problems, e.g., by using an equation with a symbol for the unknown angle measure.	Unit 8 Lessons 3, 5, 6

4.G Geometry

Draw and identify lines and angles, and classify shapes by properties of their lines and angles.

4.G.A.1	Draw points, lines, line segments, rays, angles (right, acute, obtuse), and perpendicular and parallel lines. Identify these in two-dimensional figures.	Unit 8 Lessons 1, 2, 3, 4, 5, 7, 8, 9, 10, 12
4.G.A.2	Classify two-dimensional figures based on the presence or absence of parallel or perpendicular lines, or the presence or absence of angles of a specified size. Recognize right triangles as a category, and identify right triangles.	Unit 8 Lessons 4, 8, 9, 10, 12
4.G.A.3	Recognize a line of symmetry for a two-dimensional figure as a line across the figure such that the figure can be folded along the line into matching parts. Identify line-symmetric figures and draw lines of symmetry.	Unit 8 Lessons 11, 12

■ **Major**   ■ **Supporting**   ■ **Additional**

MP1 Make sense of problems and persevere in solving them.

Mathematically proficient students start by explaining to themselves the meaning of a problem and looking for entry points to its solution. They analyze givens, constraints, relationships, and goals. They make conjectures about the form and meaning of the solution and plan a solution pathway rather than simply jumping into a solution attempt. They consider analogous problems, and try special cases and simpler forms of the original problem in order to gain insight into its solution. They monitor and evaluate their progress and change course if necessary. Older students might, depending on the context of the problem, transform algebraic expressions or change the viewing window on their graphing calculator to get the information they need. Mathematically proficient students can explain correspondences between equations, verbal descriptions, tables, and graphs or draw diagrams of important features and relationships, graph data, and search for regularity or trends. Younger students might rely on using concrete objects or pictures to help conceptualize and solve a problem. Mathematically proficient students check their answers to problems using a different method, and they continually ask themselves, "Does this make sense?" They can understand the approaches of others to solving complex problems and identify correspondences between different approaches.

Unit 1 Lessons 2, 5, 6, 7, 8, 10, 11, 12, 13, 14
Unit 2 Lessons 2, 3, 4, 5, 6, 7, 10, 11, 13, 14, 15, 16, 17, 18, 19
Unit 3 Lessons 2, 5, 6, 7, 8, 9, 10, 11
Unit 4 Lessons 2, 3, 4, 5, 6, 7, 8, 9, 12
Unit 5 Lessons 1, 2, 3, 4, 5, 6, 7, 8
Unit 6 Lessons 5, 6, 7, 10
Unit 7 Lessons 1, 2, 3, 4, 5, 6, 7, 8, 9, 10, 11, 13
Unit 8 Lessons 5, 6, 7, 8, 12

MP2 Reason abstractly and quantitatively.

Mathematically proficient students make sense of quantities and their relationships in problem situations. They bring two complementary abilities to bear on problems involving quantitative relationships: the ability to *decontextualize*—to abstract a given situation and represent it symbolically and manipulate the representing symbols as if they have a life of their own, without necessarily attending to their referents— and the ability to *contextualize*, to pause as needed during the manipulation process in order to probe into the referents for the symbols involved. Quantitative reasoning entails habits of creating a coherent representation of the problem at hand; considering the units involved; attending to the meaning of quantities, not just how to compute them; and knowing and flexibly using different properties of operations and objects.

Unit 1 Lessons 1, 3, 4, 5, 6, 8, 9, 14
Unit 2 Lessons 2, 4, 5, 6, 7, 8, 9, 10, 11, 13, 15, 16, 17, 19
Unit 3 Lessons 1, 3, 5, 7, 8, 11
Unit 4 Lessons 1, 2, 3, 4, 5, 6, 12
Unit 5 Lessons 2, 6, 7, 8
Unit 6 Lessons 1, 2, 3, 4, 7, 10
Unit 7 Lessons 1, 2, 9, 10, 13
Unit 8 Lessons 3, 5, 6, 12

MP3 Construct viable arguments and critique the reasoning of others.

Mathematically proficient students understand and use stated assumptions, definitions, and previously established results in constructing arguments. They make conjectures and build a logical progression of statements to explore the truth of their conjectures. They are able to analyze situations by breaking them into cases, and can recognize and use counterexamples. They justify their conclusions, communicate them to others, and respond to the arguments of others. They reason inductively about data, making plausible arguments that take into account the context from which the data arose. Mathematically proficient students are also able to compare the effectiveness of two plausible arguments, distinguish correct logic or reasoning from that which is flawed, and—if there is a flaw in an argument—explain what it is. Elementary students can construct arguments using concrete referents such as objects, drawings, diagrams, and actions. Such arguments can make sense and be correct, even though they are not generalized or made formal until later grades. Later, students learn to determine domains to which an argument applies. Students at all grades can listen or read the arguments of others, decide whether they make sense, and ask useful questions to clarify or improve the arguments.

Unit 1 Lessons 1, 2, 3, 4, 5, 6, 7, 8, 9, 10, 11, 12, 13, 14
Unit 2 Lessons 1, 2, 3, 4, 5, 6, 7, 8, 9, 10, 11, 12, 13, 14, 15, 16, 17, 18, 19
Unit 3 Lessons 1, 2, 3, 4, 5, 6, 7, 8, 9, 10, 11
Unit 4 Lessons 1, 2, 3, 4, 5, 6, 7, 8, 9, 10, 11, 12
Unit 5 Lessons 1, 2, 3, 4, 5, 6, 7, 8
Unit 6 Lessons 1, 2, 3, 4, 5, 6, 7, 8, 9, 10
Unit 7 Lessons 1, 2, 3, 4, 5, 6, 7, 8, 9, 10, 11, 12, 13
Unit 8 Lessons 1, 2, 3, 4, 5, 6, 7, 8, 9, 10, 11, 12

MP4 Model with mathematics.

Mathematically proficient students can apply the mathematics they know to solve problems arising in everyday life, society, and the workplace. In early grades, this might be as simple as writing an addition equation to describe a situation. In middle grades, a student might apply proportional reasoning to plan a school event or analyze a problem in the community. By high school, a student might use geometry to solve a design problem or use a function to describe how one quantity of interest depends on another. Mathematically proficient students who can apply what they know are comfortable making assumptions and approximations to simplify a complicated situation, realizing that these may need revision later. They are able to identify important quantities in a practical situation and map their relationships using such tools as diagrams, two-way tables, graphs, flowcharts and formulas. They can analyze those relationships mathematically to draw conclusions. They routinely interpret their mathematical results in the context of the situation and reflect on whether the results make sense, possibly improving the model if it has not served its purpose.

Unit 1 Lessons 1, 2, 3, 4, 6, 9, 10, 12, 13, 14
Unit 2 Lessons 1, 2, 4, 5, 6, 7, 8, 12, 16, 19
Unit 3 Lessons 1, 3, 4, 10, 11
Unit 4 Lessons 2, 3, 4, 5, 8, 9, 10, 12
Unit 5 Lessons 4, 7, 8
Unit 6 Lessons 1, 3, 4, 5, 6, 7, 8, 10
Unit 7 Lessons 2, 3, 5, 7, 8, 10, 13
Unit 8 Lessons 6, 12

MP5 Use appropriate tools strategically.

Mathematically proficient students consider the available tools when solving a mathematical problem. These tools might include pencil and paper, concrete models, a ruler, a protractor, a calculator, a spreadsheet, a computer algebra system, a statistical package, or dynamic geometry software. Proficient students are sufficiently familiar with tools appropriate for their grade or course to make sound decisions about when each of these tools might be helpful, recognizing both the insight to be gained and their limitations. For example, mathematically proficient high school students analyze graphs of functions and solutions generated using a graphing calculator. They detect possible errors by strategically using estimation and other mathematical knowledge. When making mathematical models, they know that technology can enable them to visualize the results of varying assumptions, explore consequences, and compare predictions with data. Mathematically proficient students at various grade levels are able to identify relevant external mathematical resources, such as digital content located on a website, and use them to pose or solve problems. They are able to use technological tools to explore and deepen their understanding of concepts.

Unit 1 Lessons 1, 2, 3, 4, 6, 9, 14
Unit 2 Lessons 1, 4, 5, 6, 7, 8, 10, 11, 12, 16, 19
Unit 3 Lessons 3, 4, 11
Unit 4 Lessons 2, 10, 12
Unit 5 Lessons 1, 4, 5, 6, 7, 8
Unit 6 Lessons 1, 2, 3, 4, 8, 9, 10
Unit 7 Lessons 1, 2, 4, 5, 9, 10, 11, 12, 13
Unit 8 Lessons 1, 2, 4, 5, 7, 8, 9, 10, 11, 12

MP6 Attend to precision.

Mathematically proficient students try to communicate precisely to others. They try to use clear definitions in discussion with others and in their own reasoning. They state the meaning of the symbols they choose, including using the equal sign consistently and appropriately. They are careful about specifying units of measure, and labeling axes to clarify the correspondence with quantities in a problem. They calculate accurately and efficiently, expressing numerical answers with a degree of precision appropriate for the problem context. In the elementary grades, students give carefully formulated explanations to each other. By the time they reach high school they have learned to examine claims and make explicit use of definitions.

Unit 1 Lessons 1, 2, 3, 4, 5, 6, 7, 8, 9, 10, 11, 12, 13, 14
Unit 2 Lessons 1, 2, 3, 4, 5, 6, 7, 8, 9, 10, 11, 12, 13, 14, 15, 16, 17, 18, 19
Unit 3 Lessons 1, 2, 3, 4, 5, 6, 7, 8, 9, 10, 11
Unit 4 Lessons 1, 2, 3, 4, 5, 6, 7, 8, 9, 10, 11, 12
Unit 5 Lessons 1, 2, 3, 4, 5, 6, 7, 8
Unit 6 Lessons 1, 2, 3, 4, 5, 6, 7, 8, 9, 10
Unit 7 Lessons 1, 2, 3, 4, 5, 6, 7, 8, 9, 10, 11, 12, 13
Unit 8 Lessons 1, 2, 3, 4, 5, 6, 7, 8, 9, 10, 11, 12

Common Core State Standards for Mathematical Practice

MP7 Look for and make use of structure.

Mathematically proficient students look closely to discern a pattern or structure. Young students, for example, might notice that three and seven more is the same amount as seven and three more, or they may sort a collection of shapes according to how many sides the shapes have. Later, students will see 7×8 equals the well-remembered $7 \times 5 + 7 \times 3$, in preparation for learning about the distributive property. In the expression $x^2 + 9x + 14$, older students can see the 14 as 2×7 and the 9 as $2 + 7$. They recognize the significance of an existing line in a geometric figure and can use the strategy of drawing an auxiliary line for solving problems. They also can step back for an overview and shift perspective. They can see complicated things, such as some algebraic expressions, as single objects or as being composed of several objects. For example, they can see $5 - 3(x - y)^2$ as 5 minus a positive number times a square and use that to realize that its value cannot be more than 5 for any real numbers x and y.

Unit 1 Lessons 1, 2, 4, 9, 13, 14
Unit 2 Lessons 2, 3, 6, 8, 9, 10, 13, 16, 17, 19
Unit 3 Lessons 1, 3, 10, 11
Unit 4 Lessons 1, 2, 3, 5, 10, 11, 12
Unit 5 Lessons 1, 2, 4, 8
Unit 6 Lessons 1, 4, 5, 10
Unit 7 Lessons 2, 6, 9, 10, 11, 12, 13
Unit 8 Lessons 1, 2, 4, 7, 8, 9, 10

MP8 Look for and express regularity in repeated reasoning.

Mathematically proficient students notice if calculations are repeated, and look both for general methods and for shortcuts. Upper elementary students might notice when dividing 25 by 11 that they are repeating the same calculations over and over again, and conclude they have a repeating decimal. By paying attention to the calculation of slope as they repeatedly check whether points are on the line through (1, 2) with slope 3, middle school students might abstract the equation $(y - 2)/(x - 1) = 3$. Noticing the regularity in the way terms cancel when expanding $(x - 1)(x + 1)$, $(x - 1)(x^2 + x + 1)$, and $(x - 1)(x^3 + x^2 + x + 1)$ might lead them to the general formula for the sum of a geometric series. As they work to solve a problem, mathematically proficient students maintain oversight of the process, while attending to the details. They continually evaluate the reasonableness of their intermediate results.

Unit 1 Lessons 3, 4, 5, 6, 7, 10, 11, 14
Unit 2 Lessons 1, 2, 3, 5, 7, 8, 15, 17, 19
Unit 3 Lessons 1, 3, 5, 6, 11
Unit 4 Lessons 1, 2, 10, 11, 12
Unit 5 Lessons 1, 4, 6, 8
Unit 6 Lessons 2, 7, 9, 10
Unit 7 Lessons 1, 3, 6, 8, 10, 11, 13
Unit 8 Lessons 1, 3, 4, 9, 10, 11, 12

© Houghton Mifflin Harcourt Publishing Company

Index

E

© Houghton Mifflin Harcourt Publishing Company

Index

© Houghton Mifflin Harcourt Publishing Company

Index

pictograph, 177
  vertical bar, 178
horizontal bar, 39–40
line plot, 220, 272, 284, 319–320
pictograph, 177
pie, 283
vertical bar, 178

Greater than (>), 10, 13, 257–258, 267, 297–298, 315–317, 327, 331, 336, 359

H

Hundreds
modeling, 3
Hundredths, 325, 329

I

Inch, 223–224, 233, 235, 272
Inequality. *See also* Algebra, inequalities.
is not equal to (≠) sign, 163
Interpret remainders, 143–144, 185
Inverse operations
addition and subtraction, 29–30, 38, 164
multiplication and division, 117, 167
Isosceles triangle, 365–368, 390–392

K

Kilogram, 217–218
Kiloliter, 215
Kilometer, 212–214

L

Length. *See also* Measurement.
area, 53, 232–234, 236, 237
customary units, 223–224
fractions of units, 224
metric units, 211–214
perimeter, 231, 233–234, 236, 237
of sides, 53, 231–234

Less than (<), 10, 13, 257–258, 297–298, 315–317, 331, 336
Line, 351, 379–382, 391–392
Line of symmetry, 397–400
Line plot
analyze, 220, 272, 284, 319–320
make, 220, 272, 320
Line segment, 351, 379–382, 391–392
Line symmetry, 397–400
Liquid volume, 215–216, 218, 227–228
Liter, 215–216, 218, 235

M

Manipulatives
Fraction Bars, 260A
Fraction Strips, 266A–266B
Polygon Cards, 396A
Quadrilateral Cutouts, 386A
Secret Code Cards
  Decimal, 330A–330B, 334A–334B
  Whole Number, 6A–6D
Maps, 337, 358, 382
Mass, measurement of, 217–218, 235
Measurement
angles, 355–360, 370, 373–374
area and arrays, 53–54, 232–234, 236, 237–238. *See also* Area models; Arrays.
area and perimeter, 231–234, 236, 237–238. *See also* Area; Perimeter.
find unknown measures, 234, 236, 237–238
formulas, 233
rectangles, 53–54, 231–234, 236, 237–238
choose appropriate unit, 212
circle
  angles in, 355, 359–360, 373
customary, S3–S4
  area, 233–234, 236, 237
  convert units, 223–224, 225–228, 235
  length, 223–224, 228, 235
    foot, 223

Index

Rectangle Model, 53–54, 56, 61–62, 65, 67–68, 69–70, 71, 75–76, 85–86, 87, 95–96, 97

Shortcut Method, 74, 88, 91, 97–98

money, 63–64, 78

multiples, 57–58, 65, 119, 193–194, 213–214, 215–218, 316

one-digit by four-digit, 95–96, 97–101

one-digit by three-digit, 75–78

patterns, 55, 57–58, 119, 194, 195

properties of

Associative Property, 55

Commutative Property, 55

Distributive Property, 69

relate to division, 117, 119, 121, 167

two-digit by one-digit, 54, 61–66, 65–66, 67–68, 69–70, 71–72, 73–74

two-digit by two-digit, 55–56, 85–86, 87–88, 89–90, 91–92

write equations, 61, 167–168, 171–172, 175–176, 277–278, 280–282

with zeros, 119

Multiplicative comparison, 171–172, 175–176

Multistep problems, 81–82, 146, 183–188

N

New Groups Above Method

1-Row Product, in multiplication, 74

in addition, 17, 19

New Groups Below Method

1-Row Product, in multiplication, 74, 88

in addition, 17, 19

Number line(s)

benchmarks, 301–302

to compare decimals, 329

to compare fractions, 299–301

to convert units of measures, 214, 215–218, 223, 227, 228

fraction on, 299–301, 315

mixed numbers on, 300

represent data on, 220

Numbers

compare, 10, 13, 257, 258, 297–298, 336

composite, 192, 194

decimal, 325–327

decimals on a number line, 329

even, 58, 192

format

expanded form, 8, 14

standard form, 8

word form, 8

fractions on a number line, 299–301

grouping, 17, 19

identifying, 7, 11

odd, 195

ordering, 258

patterns, 7, 195

prime, 192

reading, 11–12

representing, 3–7, 220

rounding, 8, 14, 21, 99, 141

Secret Code Cards, 7, 11, 329–334, 334

writing, 8, 12

Numerator, 251

O

Obtuse angle, 359–360, 367–368, 371, 382, 387–388, 395

Obtuse triangle, 363–364, 367–368, 387–388

Order of Operations, 161, 163, 183–188

Ounce, 225

P

Parallel lines, 379, 381–382

Parallelogram, 387–390

rectangle, 231–234, 236, 385–386

rhombus, 385–386

square, 233, 385–386, 401

Partial products, 69

Partitioning, 212

Patterns

extending, 195–196

in fraction bars, 252

in multiplication, 57, 193–194

growing, 196

numerical patterns, 195

Index

Timeline, 12

Trapezoid, 384

Triangle. *See also* **Geometry.**
acute, 363–364, 367–368, 387–388, 390
classify, 367–368, 395, 396A
equilateral, 365–368, 387–388, 390
identify, 364–368, 387–388, 390
isosceles, 365–368, 387–388, 390
name, 364–368, 387–390
obtuse, 363–364, 367–368, 387–388, 390
from quadrilaterals, 387–390
right, 363–364, 367–368, 387–388,
    390–392
scalene, 365–368, 387–388, 390
sorting, 367–368, 395, 396

U

Ungrouping, with zeros, 27–28

Unit Fractions, 251. *See also* **Fractions.**
addition of, 251
comparing, 257
multiplication of, 251
multiplication of whole numbers by, 275
ordering, 258

V

Variable, 33, 161–162, 165–168

Vertex
of angle, 352, 358, 365, 370, 391–392
of polygon, 391–392

Volume. *See* **Liquid volume.**

Weight, 217, 225–226, 228, 235

**What's the Error? 38, 82, 90, 100, 130,
134, 139, 166, 176, 186, 216, 258, 261,
268, 270, 278, 297, 301, 310, 317, 372,
392, 399**

Width, 232

Word form, 8

Word Problems
division, 128, 135–136, 140, 144, 145–146,
    147–148
fractions, 271, 277–278, 280, 282, 304
intervals of time, 221–222
measurement, 235–236
missing information, 80
mixed, 36–37, 145–146
multistep, 40, 79–82, 146, 185–188, 235
one-step, 145, 179, 182
subtraction, 30, 32–33, 34, 37
too much or too little information, 79–80
two-step, 181–182

Y

Yard, 223

Z

Zero
divide with, 119–121
in greater decimal numbers, 335
multiply with, 95

...Brill

...to use shapes to draw animals like the lemur on the cover?

Over the last 10 years Josh has been using geometric shapes to design his a nimals. His aim is to keep the animal drawings simple and use color to make them appealing.

Add some color to the lemur Josh drew. Then try drawing a cat or dog or some other animal using the shapes below.

Shape Toolbox